CHICKEN DIY

Daniel Johnson
and
Samantha Johnson

Chicken **DIY**

CompanionHouse Books™ is an imprint of Fox Chapel Publishers International Ltd.

Project Team
Vice President–Content: Christopher Reggio
Editor: Amy Deputato
Copy Editor: Laura Taylor
Design: Mary Ann Kahn
Index: Amy Deputato

ISBN 978-1-62008-230-0

Library of Congress Cataloging-in-Publication Data
Names: Johnson, Samantha, author. | Johnson, Daniel, 1984- author.
Title: Chicken DIY : 20 fun-to-build projects for happy, healthy chickens /
   Samantha Johnson and Daniel Johnson.
Description: Mount Joy, PA : Fox Chapel Publishing, [2017] | Includes index.
   Identifiers: LCCN 2017044744 (print) | LCCN 2017047391 (ebook) | ISBN
   9781620082270 () | ISBN 9781620082300 (softcover)
Subjects: LCSH: Chickens. | Do-it-yourself work.
Classification: LCC SF487 (ebook) | LCC SF487 .J67 2017 (print) | DDC
   636.5--dc23
LC record available at https://lccn.loc.gov/2017044744

This book has been published with the intent to provide accurate and authoritative information in regard to the subject matter within. While every precaution has been taken in the preparation of this book, the author and publisher expressly disclaim any responsibility for any errors, omissions, or adverse effects arising from the use or application of the information contained herein. The techniques and suggestions are used at the reader's discretion and are not to be considered a substitute for veterinary care. If you suspect a medical problem, consult your veterinarian.

Fox Chapel Publishing
903 Square Street
Mount Joy, PA 17552

Fox Chapel Publishers International Ltd.
7 Danefield Road, Selsey (Chichester)
West Sussex PO20 9DA, U.K.

www.facebook.com/companionhousebooks

We are always looking for talented authors. To submit an idea, please send a brief inquiry to acquisitions@foxchapelpublishing.com.

Printed and bound in Singapore
20 19 18 17   2 4 6 8 10 9 7 5 3 1

Contents

Introduction

Happy chickens will make you happy, too!

Welcome! We're pretty sure that we know why you've chosen this particular book: you keep, or you're planning to keep, a flock of chickens, and you also enjoy the idea of creating and constructing things. You're definitely not alone—chickens are one of the most popular livestock options for small-scale and hobby farm operations.

And why not? Chickens are generally easy to care for and inexpensive to keep, they can be raised in small backyards as well as on larger properties. The required infrastructure for a flock of chickens—housing, fencing, and feeding/watering equipment—is minimal and well within the reach of a DIYer who would like the satisfaction of building these items for him- or herself.

That's where this book comes in. Our goal is to provide you with a jumping-off place for a series of projects that can be put to good use in your chicken farming. From a portable chicken tractor and collapsible grazing pen to chicken creature comforts, like a wading pool and dust-bathing area, to a few projects that focus on fun, these projects aim to offer the reader a wide variety of directions to pursue.

Feel free to follow our directions to the letter or modify aspects to your own liking. In many cases, the cost of project materials is quite low, and many of the projects can be made almost entirely from scrap materials that a seasoned DIYer might already have on hand ("I knew that 2-foot piece of 2x4 would come in handy!").

We hope that you find plenty of inspiration and help throughout the pages of this book. And after trying a few of these projects, you'll end up with something to crow about! Happy building!

In addition to the fun and satisfaction that comes from raising chickens, the potential for fresh eggs is a major attraction for many chicken owners.

Looking for a wonderful project in which the whole family can participate? Why not keep chickens?

Chapter 1

Why DIY?

The duties of a DIY chicken keeper are many, but the rewards are well worth the effort!

Maybe you're already a DIY enthusiast with a track record of producing some pretty awesome results around the house. Maybe you love the idea of creating helpful, useful items for outside your home, too.

For many people, there are rewards to be found in constructing nest boxes and roosts and grazing boxes—satisfaction in the ability to be self-sufficient and enterprising as well as joy in the task of construction itself. But some people question the purpose of DIY projects. "Hey! Why are you using scrap wood to make your chicken gear when you could just go purchase many of these items from a retailer?"

The answer will vary from person to person, but here are some common answers to the question "Why DIY?"

Saving Money

It goes without saying that if you can build something yourself from materials you already have sitting around, you can save a lot of money compared to going out and buying the manufactured version of the same item. Even if you have to purchase some or all of the supplies to build something on your own, it's likely that you'll still enjoy significant savings since you won't be paying for someone else's time (and price markup).

You'll find plenty of satisfaction in using your own skills and tools to produce quality equipment for your small-scale chicken operation.

Doing it yourself can be a real money saver, and you'll also have the ability to customize the projects to your own preferences.

Of course, there's a trade-off: you'll need to invest your own time in each project, but if you're thrifty and make good use of your materials, you might be able to complete several projects for very little financial output.

Recycling

As the saying goes, "One person's trash is another person's treasure." Along with saving money, DIY projects can also save items from winding up in a landfill. Remember those leftover scraps of wood from building your chicken coop—the ones stacked up in the tool shed? Maybe they're too short and oddly shaped to be of any use—or maybe they're perfect for constructing a collapsible chicken run. What about that 5-gallon bucket that leaks and no longer holds water? Maybe it's time to throw it away—or maybe it's time to turn it into a nest box.

The ability to take an item that was destined for the trash and turn it into something useful is certainly an appealing aspect of DIY projects. If you're the type of person who likes to hang on to scraps for future use, DIY chicken projects might be the perfect way for you to put those materials to good use and save some money at the same time.

Customization

By taking the DIY route, you also have the ability to customize projects to suit your personal preference and needs. Let's say your coop is custom-made or part of a larger building. Imagine the convenience of being able to construct nest boxes, roosts, feeders, and waterers to a very specific size or design—what a great benefit!

Your happy chickens will thank you for your efforts, and you'll enjoy the process, too.

DIY projects are an excellent way to use up scrap materials left over from other projects. Don't throw the material away—reuse it!

Satisfaction

While it might be easy to go down to the farm-supply store and buy a chicken feeder, you really can't underestimate the personal satisfaction that comes from building things yourself. It's vastly rewarding to visit your chicken coop each day and see your chickens using the items that you've built with your own two hands. It's hard to put a price on satisfaction like that!

Are You Ready to Start?

By following the steps outlined in this book, you will soon be well equipped with an impressive variety of chicken-related products that will transform your coop and its surroundings into a chicken paradise. But as much as anything else, the projects in this book were conceived as inspiration for your own DIY ideas. While we certainly recommend that you follow the steps provided herein, we also encourage you to modify the designs to fit your individual needs, as long as you always keep your chickens' safety (and your own safety) first and foremost in your mind.

Important!

Metric conversions for measurements in the projects are close approximations, so please double-check the measurements before obtaining materials for each project. Also, some measurements, such as "2x4" are common instead of actual measurements. In these cases, the metric conversions are based on the actual, rather than the common, measurements.

Chapter 2

Basic Tools and Skills

R eady to do some construction? Great! But do you have the equipment and knowledge you need to complete the job? Photos, step-by-step directions, and cut lists are helpful, but unless you have the tools and know-how to put them to use, DIY projects can prove challenging. Here are some basic tools and skills you'll need to create the projects in this book.

Basic Tools

At the start of each project, we'll supply you with a list of the tools needed for that particular job. But, as a brief overview, here are some of the tools you'll want to have on hand.

Hammer

For your basic nailing, tapping, and prying, the classic claw hammer is the tool you need. We recommend a simple 16-ounce hammer because this size strikes a nice balance between functionality and effectiveness.

Electric Drill

These days, when we say electric drill, we're really talking about a modern cordless drill—lightweight, easy to use, and fully portable. This tool allows you to do everything from drilling large holes through wood to pre-drilling nail holes for hand-nailing to installing and removing short and long screws while assembling large projects. Basically, it's a must-have tool and probably our favorite of all.

When purchasing a drill, consider the drill's power versus its weight. A 14-volt drill might be easy to handle, but it might not have the strength for some of the tasks in the projects (particularly fastening 2x4s with long screws). Drills upward of 20 volts have more power, but they're bulkier and heavier. Before you make a final selection, try out a few sizes to see what feels comfortable to you. Bonus tip: It's a good idea to purchase two batteries so that you can be using one while charging the other. Trust us—this scenario happens more than you expect.

Hammer

Drill

Circular Saw

This is one of the most popular and common power saws, and it's a workhorse for many carpenters. A circular saw is lightweight and easy to handle with a small-but-useful blade (7¼ inches is the most common size), which makes it the perfect choice for many general-purpose cutting tasks. Like the electric drill, a circular saw is essentially a must-have item for carpentry work.

You can find circular saws that use rechargeable batteries, but these saws might be a little underpowered for some of the tasks you'll throw at it, and you may prefer a corded (although admittedly less convenient) version.

Jigsaw

A jigsaw features a narrow, vertical blade that rapidly saws up and down, allowing the user to make fine, careful, precise cuts, although slowly. You won't need a jigsaw often, but when a task requires one, there is really no better option.

Miter Saw or Chop Saw

Okay, let's say you have something repetitive and tedious to do, like sawing a long series of 2x4s to the same length. You can always do this with a circular saw, but it will require repeated measuring and marking of each 2x4 and many careful cuts with the circular saw. A miter saw or chop saw can take a lot of the effort out of this job—you just set up the length you need, and then you can saw each 2x4 one after another, which saves time. (Curious about the difference? A miter saw can cut various angles, while a chop saw can do only 90° angles.)

Circular saw

Jigsaw

Miter Saw

Miter Saw

Table saw

Table saw

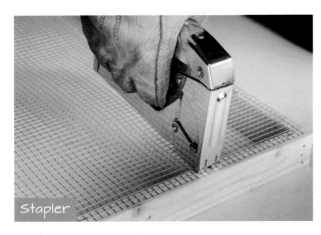

Stapler

Wire Snippers

Table Saw

It's one thing to make a quick cut across the narrow side of a board; for example, to modify a 10-foot 2x8 into a 6-foot 2x8. A circular saw can do this job—called a *cross cut*—quickly and simply. But it's quite another problem to *rip* that same board; that is, to make a long, straight cut up the middle, parallel to the grain. It's possible to do a cut like this using a circular saw with a rip guide, but it's time-consuming and difficult and will likely lead to wobbly results. A table saw is the solution here because it allows you to easily feed a long section of lumber through a guide-aided blade that will rip the boards to the exact width you need.

Stapler

A handheld staple gun is a great time-saver for the many projects that require hardware cloth or screening. While it's possible to attach hardware cloth or a screen using other methods (such as nailing), a stapler and a box of $\frac{5}{16}$-inch staples are handy tools to have in your box.

Wire Snippers

Speaking of hardware cloth, you'll need a way to cut out sections of specific dimensions for use in the projects. A solid pair of wire snippers (they're sometimes called tin snippers or aviation snips) can be an excellent tool for this use.

General Safety Warning

It goes without saying that any activity involving construction and assembly using hand or power tools should be approached with due caution and safety in mind, and these DIY chicken projects are no exception. Always use caution when working on any construction; project; safety should be the main priority. Pay attention to your task and your surroundings—including curious "onlookers." Read manuals and learn the safest ways to operate your tools, and don't ever place yourself in danger while working. Many of the activities detailed in this book have the potential to be dangerous, and failure to exercise proper safety behaviors could result in injury or death. The authors cannot assume responsibility for any damage to property or injury to persons as a result of the use or misuse of the information provided.

Carpentry Supplies

In addition to the tools, you'll want to keep the following carpentry supplies on hand.

Pencil

From taking notes, writing down measurements, and making your all-important cut marks for sawing, a durable pencil (or two!) is critical for your DIY projects. A carpentry pencil is your best bet because the extra thickness helps you make bold lines.

Tape Measure

Never go into a woodworking project without a high-quality tape measure. A 16-foot tape measure is probably suitable for most of the projects in this book, but 25 feet is standard and is a general, all-purpose size, so opt for a 25-foot version if you can.

Level

Most of these DIY projects won't require super-high precision, but, with that said, a carpenter's level can be very helpful when you need to keep something perfectly level (straight horizontally) or plumb (straight vertically). You'll find many uses for a small 2-foot level, but you may also want a longer 4-foot or 6-foot level as well.

A tape measure, pencil, and square in use.

Sawhorses

Square

Here's the key to carpentry tasks: keeping things straight. A framing square can help you with this task, especially when working with larger jobs. A smaller 6-inch speed square is great for quick jobs. And either one can double as a ruler.

Sawhorses

You'll need a place up off the ground to make cuts and assemble the projects, and a simple pair of sawhorses can help with this and more. Sawhorses also make for an all-around portable work table. Sawhorses can be made of wood, metal, or even plastic; we've found that the plastic sawhorses can be quite effective and easy to use for lightweight projects.

Safety Gear

DIY projects are only fun when they're safe. Keep yourself safe by wearing safety glasses, a dust mask, and ear protection whenever you need to. Gloves are also critical for some tasks, especially when moving lumber and materials around or working with hardware cloth and other sharp items. Have extra safety gear handy for the inevitable spectators who come to watch you in action.

Ear, eye, and breathing protection

Basic Skills

The goal of this book is to present some ideas for simple carpentry/craft projects that don't require high precision. Still, your completed DIY projects can only be as good as your skills allow. Here are some of the techniques that you'll need to be able to do (or at least do with help).

Nailing

To be honest, these projects require very little nailing, aside from perhaps tacking down hardware cloth with roofing nails, but it's still important to be able to handle a hammer properly and effectively. An air nailer will be quite helpful for some projects, especially those involving extra precision and delicacy, but this tool is an additional expense and requires an air compressor to function.

Nailing Tips

Don't try to put a nail in too close to the edge of the wood, or the wood may split. Also avoid nailing into knots in the wood because knots are amazingly hard and thus difficult to nail into.

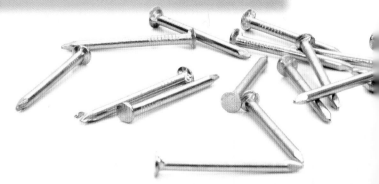

Screwing

For most of the actual construction aspects of these projects, we usually recommend using an electric drill and fastening the components with screws. Screwing—especially for beginners—is probably easier and faster than nailing. Work slowly with the drill at the beginning until you get a feel for it—don't rush. You can control the speed of the drill with the trigger, which will allow you to start a screw at a low speed and then work faster as the screw digs in deeper into the wood.

Cross Cuts

A cross cut is when you cut a piece of wood across the grain, and this is most likely what you have in mind when you think of cutting wood. You'll make many cross cuts while working on these projects, especially when cutting sections of 2x4s to length. You can use either a circular saw or a chop/miter saw for cross cuts.

Rip Cuts

The opposite of a cross cut, a rip cut goes *with* the grain of the wood—a bit like a sawmill. Rip cuts can be useful when modifying sections of plywood or other boards or any time you need to make narrow strips of wood. It's possible to use a circular saw to make a rip cut here and there, but it's best to use a table saw.

Measuring and Marking

So you probably know all about "Measure twice, cut once," but that old advice is very true: it's quite easy to make measuring and marking mistakes, ruining wood for your project and wasting time. Our advice? Take it slow, get familiar with your tape measure, and make bold marks. And then check them again before you make your cuts.

Making a cross cut with a circular saw.

Preparing to make a rip cut with a table saw.

Remember:
Get Help When You Need It

The carpentry skills required for the projects in this book are fairly simple on the whole. While there may be the occasional task or step that is more demanding, we have, for the most part, tried to avoid overly advanced techniques. Likewise, most of the projects can be completed with tools that the average DIYer already possesses or can easily borrow.

But here's something we want you to always keep in mind: get help and advice when you need it. If you would like to complete a particular project but aren't sure about how to accomplish one or more of the steps, or if you need help on a trickier skill, don't hesitate to request help from someone with more extensive experience. A more advanced DIYer might have the knowledge and tools needed for certain tasks, which can make the difference between successfully completing a project or just becoming discouraged.

Chapter 3

A Look at the History of Chicken Keeping

Like most things, the art and science of chicken keeping has come a long way over the past century. As knowledge of chicken health and nutrition has improved, our feathery friends have gone from living almost wild to thriving in specially built coops where they are doted on daily. Suffice to say, modern-day chickens raised by small-time chicken keepers live a life of luxury in comparison to their distant ancestors from the early 1900s.

Of course, the history of chicken keeping goes back even further than that. Despite the vast number of chickens that currently reside in the United States—approximately 280 million—these birds aren't native to North America. We can credit Christopher Columbus for introducing the continent to Europe, but we are also indebted to him for introducing chickens to the New World.

But even with a legendary historical figure helping chickens cross the globe, chickens generally haven't had it easy throughout history. Back around the turn of the twentieth century, when airplanes were just starting to take flight and television had yet to be invented, farmers who kept chickens did so with small flocks that were generally left to fend for themselves. These flocks lived primarily outdoors—making predators a bigger threat—and the chickens' diets were far from regimented; they generally ate whatever they could find plus a few extras (leftovers) provided by their keepers. This free-for-all meant that the highest-ranking members of the chickens' social society got the most food.

Historically, free-ranging was the norm for chickens, but this made them more vulnerable to predators than they are today.

Over the years, technology has improved and provides new options for chicken keepers Here, a simple solar panel supplies power for an electric fence to help keep chickens safe.

Chicken coops weren't very elaborate either, and chicken diseases were poorly understood. Essentially, if you were a chicken in the olden days, you could expect a short lifespan.

Fortunately, change was just around the corner. As scientific knowledge improved in leaps and bounds, so did the health of chickens. One breakthrough came with the realization that chickens needed plenty of vitamin D in order to remain healthy during the winter, and efforts to keep chickens during the winter were significantly improved with the addition of extra vitamin D to their diets.

World War II also had an impact on chicken keeping in the United States, perhaps even accelerating the development of improved chicken-raising techniques.

Today's chicken keepers sometimes free-range their birds on a more limited basis, usually opting to return the birds to the coop at night.

Modern housing for chickens strikes a balance between practicality (for the flock) and beauty (for the landscape).

As the government promoted chicken keeping (primarily of laying hens) as a patriotic task that would produce eggs for the country, the stage was set for the industry to grow to greater heights.

Around the same time, a change in chickens' living quarters also made a difference for their health. By the time the 1950s rolled around, chickens were being kept primarily in their coops, where they were safer from predators and could be fed diets that were more carefully controlled. Furthermore, experiments with housing chickens above the ground (as opposed to letting them live on the ground) improved the cleanliness of the average coop, reducing disease (and keeping eggs cleaner, too).

As chicken keeping has continued to gain popularity, many more improvements have been made. Nowadays, our backyard chickens live pampered lives of luxury (some might even say that we spoil them). Our custom-designed coops provide our chickens with everything they need to thrive, and our chickens enjoy an idyllic existence. Our chickens are protected from predators, provided with entertainment (chicken swing, anyone?), and outfitted in the latest chicken-sweater fashions.

It's a great time to be involved with chickens, and we hope this book helps you keep your flock happy and healthy. Congratulations—you're about to start writing your own chapter in the history of chicken keeping!

Chapter 4

The Projects

Chicken Tractor

Level of Difficulty: Intermediate
Length of Time: 3 hours

For many chicken keepers, the prospect of free-ranging birds is appealing because it's a way to offer a more natural lifestyle for their chickens. The downside to free-ranging is that the chickens are more vulnerable to predators and accidents, along with the fact that the birds may free-range into areas where you may not want them, such as lawns or porches.

A chicken tractor can help bridge the gap between confinement and free-ranging. Essentially a portable chicken run, a chicken tractor is a simple structure that is wired off to protect the chickens but still offers some form of shade. Some chicken tractors can be quite elaborate, complete with roosts and nest boxes, but the following design is for a basic chicken tractor that is intended for daytime use in warm weather. The goal was to build a chicken tractor that could be constructed mostly out of scrap material. It's a great way to use up some shorter sections of 2x4 (38 x 89 mm) and other lumber that might not be useful otherwise. In fact, this model was built entirely out of scrap except for the hardware cloth and fasteners, so the cost was very low.

Keep in mind that this is just one type of chicken tractor; you can easily make yours larger, smaller, longer, or shorter by making simple adjustments to the measurements. This design is reasonably lightweight for easy maneuvering—an ATV or lawn tractor, or even a couple of people, should be able to move it easily—and it should hold a handful of chickens comfortably.

MATERIALS

Cut list:
- Three 6-foot (1¾-m) 2x4s (38 x 89 mm)
- Six 3-foot (91 cm) 2x4s (38 x 89 mm)
- 34¾-inch (88-cm) 2x4 (38 x 89 mm)
- Two 35-inch (89-cm) 2x2s (38 x 38 mm)
- Twelve 7 x 37½-inch (18 x 95-cm) cedar shakes
- Six 37-inch (94-cm) cedar 1x4s (19 x 89 mm)
- 75-inch (2-m) cedar 1x4 (19 x 89 mm)

Parts list:
- 37 x 75-inch (94 cm x 2-m) section ¼-inch (6-mm) or ½-inch (13-mm) hardware cloth
- Two 33 x 33 x 33-inch (84 x 84 x 84-cm) triangles ¼-inch (6-mm) or ½-inch (12-mm) hardware cloth
- Two 3-inch (76-mm) hinges
- Hook-and-eye latch
- Box 3-inch (76-mm) exterior screws
- Box 4-inch (10-cm) exterior screws
- Box 1½-inch (38-mm) exterior screws
- Screwdriver
- Roofing nails or staples (for hardware cloth)

Tools needed:
- Framing square
- Hammer
- Chop saw or circular saw
- Level
- Stapler (if using staples)

Step 1: Build base

Assemble the tractor's footprint by creating a large rectangle out of two of the 6-foot (1¾-m) 2x4s (38 x 89 mm) and two of the 3-foot (91 cm) 2x4s (38 x 89 mm). Use screws to fasten them together, as shown. Throughout the project, using two screws per connection is usually adequate. A framing square will help you keep everything straight and square.

Step 2: Build both ends

Assemble two ends by using a chop saw or circular saw to modify the remaining four 3-foot (91 cm) 2x4s (38 x 89 mm). Make a 30-degree cut on each of the ends as shown, but notice how each of the cuts is made from a different orientation. It's important to get this correct in order for the pieces to fit together, so use the photos as a reference. Then, screw the two sets together and attach them to the lower frame to create two triangles. Use the 4-inch (10-cm) screws for connecting the triangles to the lower frame.

Step 3: Attach ridgepole

Attach the remaining 6-foot (1¾-m) 2x4 (38 x 89 mm) (the ridgepole) across the top of the chicken tractor with screws, in between the two end triangles.

Step 4: Attach hardware cloth to sides

Hardware cloth is used to give the chicken tractor plenty of ventilation and to give the chickens light while still keeping them contained to protect them from predators. Chicken wire isn't the best option because it's easily damaged by predators. Use one 37 x 75-inch (94 cm x 2-m) section and create half-length sides for the chicken tractor. (The remaining areas will be covered with a shade/shelter.) Attach with roofing nails or staples spaced about 8 inches (20 cm) apart (adjust spacing if needed to keep the hardware cloth from bowing).

Step 5: Attach hardware cloth to ends

Take two 33 x 33 x 33-inch (84 x 84 x 84-cm) triangles of hardware cloth and use them to cover the two ends of the chicken tractor. Attach from the inside (for a cleaner look) with roofing nails or staples spaced about 8 inches (20 cm) apart.

Step 6: Add braces

Install two modified 35-inch (89-cm) 2x2s (38 x 38 mm) to act as braces for the hardware cloth and shade. Like the triangular ends of the chicken tractor, you'll need to make two 30-degree cuts in the same way, as shown in the photos. Using four 1½-inch (38-mm) screws, screw these into the frame about 37 inches (94 cm) from the non-hardware-clothed end and then pin down the hardware cloth with roofing nails or staples.

Step 7: Attach shade

You can create the shade portion of your chicken tractor out of whatever you have handy. We used some scrap cedar shakes that were long enough for the job (37½ inches [95 cm]) and around 7 inches (18 cm) wide. Using 1½-inch (38-mm) screws (one or two per side should

be enough), attach these on one side of the chicken tractor. Use a level to keep everything straight.

Step 8: Add doorway

Build a door to give your chickens a way to enter and exit the chicken tractor. We used two of the cedar shakes fastened together with a couple of roofing nails, but, again, you can use other materials that you have on hand. Using four 3-inch screws, install a 34¾-inch (88-cm) 2x4 (38 x 89 mm) about 12½ inches (32 cm) up from the bottom. Two 3-inch (76-mm) hinges complete the job and create a chicken-sized door. We used four more cedar shakes to close off the remaining opening.

Step 9: Finishing touches

A few trim boards will make the chicken tractor a little nicer and cover some of the rough edges of the hardware cloth. We used some cedar 1x4s that we had handy. Use four 37-inch (94-cm) cedar 1x4s (19 x 89 mm) to trim the middle edges of the chicken tractor and the hardware cloth end. Use two more for the shaded end, but modify them on the top to 30°. You can use a 75-inch (2-m) cedar 1x4 (19 x 89 mm) as trim across the very top, although we actually used two shorter pieces.

Finally, simply add a hook-and-eye latch to keep the door shut. It's also a good idea to place a couple of handles near the bottom so you can easily attach the chicken tractor to an ATV or move the chicken tractor by hand.

Dust-Bathing Area

Level of Difficulty: Beginner
Length of Time: 1 hour

If you've been around chickens for any length of time, you've probably observed their endearing and beneficial behavior of dust bathing. When dust bathing, chickens will find an area of sand or soil, scratch out holes with their feet, and then proceed to roll and roll until they are covered with dirt and dust, which they then proceed to shake off.

First-time chicken owners sometimes think there is something wrong with their birds, but in fact the opposite is true: chickens clearly seem to enjoy dust bathing, and it even serves some practical benefits as well. Dust bathing is a chicken's way of naturally controlling external parasites, like mites, because the dust and sharp edges of the particles actually kill and smother these pests. Dust bathing is an essential part of being a chicken, and your chickens will attempt to do it whether they have an "official" designated place to do so or not.

So, if you'd like to try to encourage your hens to dig their holes where you want (not in the flower beds!), why not try building your own dust-bathing area? It's pretty simple, and your chickens (and your plants) will thank you.

These directions explain how to create one type of dust-bathing area. You can adjust the dimensions of your dust-bathing area to meet the needs of your flock, and it's easy to make adjustments because the design is so simple.

One thing to keep in mind is that if you go too shallow, the birds may end up kicking dirt out of the box (we went with 9-inch [23-cm] sides to combat this). Obviously, the larger you make your box, the more material you'll need to fill it, so plan ahead before you go overly large. People with only a few chickens have had luck with something as simple as a kitty litter box, although that's pretty small and doesn't hold much dust. The option we've described should give your chickens enough room and enough dirt to dust bathe without kicking out too much dust in the process.

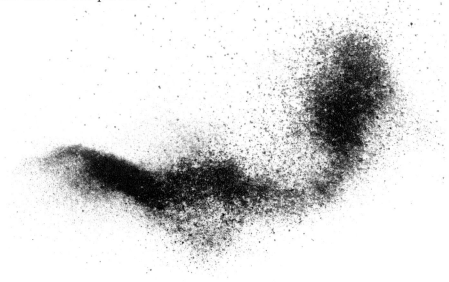

MATERIALS

Cut list:
- Four 9 x 24-inch (23 x 61-cm) pine boards

Parts list:
- 1½-inch (38-mm) nails
- Sand
- Soil
- Wood-fire ashes (optional)
- Food-grade diatomaceous earth (optional)

Tools needed:
- Circular saw
- Hammer
- Tape measure
- Carpenter's square
- Pencil

Step 1: *Make cuts*

First, prepare the pieces for the sides of your dust-bathing box. Using a tape measure and circular saw, measure and cut an 8-foot (2½-m) piece of 9-inch (23-cm) pine into four equal 24-inch (61-cm) pieces.

Step 2: *Assemble frame*

Using the four 24-inch (61-cm) segments, form a simple box frame and fasten it on all corners with 1½-inch (38-mm) nails.

Step 3: *Add dust material, part 1*

Before you add the dust material, choose a suitable place near your coop to locate your dust-bathing area; it's not easy to move later. Start adding your dust-bathing mixture. In the example photos, we've used a 50/50 mix of soil and sand, which is designed to provide the birds with a dust bath of a consistency to their liking. Chickens like a dusty, dry bath, and the sand helps provide this while being balanced by the soil. Add soil first…

Step 4: *Add dust material, part 2*

…then add the sand.

Step 5: *Mix well*

Mix the soil and sand together until you have a thorough combination.

Other Additives

There are other "dusty" options you can add to your chickens' dust-bathing mixture. Many people find that their chickens enjoy wood-fire ashes, as these are very dusty and can be a nice addition to the mixture. Be sure to only use ashes from wood fires because ashes from other types of fires (charcoal, garbage, and the like) can harm your chickens. Food-grade diatomaceous earth is another common additive for dust-bathing boxes because the particles are very sharp and are good at killing parasites. One problem is that the dust from diatomaceous earth poses a health hazard to you, so you must be careful when using it. Also, be sure to only use food-grade diatomaceous earth, not the pool-grade variety used for cleaning swimming pools.

Whatever materials you choose, use equal parts of all ingredients.

Feeder/Waterer

Level of Difficulty: Beginner
Length of Time: 1 hour

S ometimes chicken owners find themselves frustrated when trying to find an ideal feeding and watering system for their birds. "My hens tip over their food!" or "Their water is always a mess!" are common complaints. If this sounds familiar, you might want to experiment with building your own "spill-resistant" chicken feeder and "mess-resistant" waterer. Happily, these are easy projects that are within the abilities of almost any DIYer, and they're built out of common materials that don't cost much.

There are many different designs and ways to tackle this project, but most DIY feeders and waterers are just variations on the same theme. In this project, we'll show you how to assemble one version each of non-spill, easy-clean feeders and waterers, but keep in mind that these directions are easily adaptable for your own situation. For example, you may want to lengthen or shorten certain components to make them fit easily into your coop or to suit your number of chickens. You might also want to add components so that you can fill the feeder and waterer from outside the coop to avoid having to enter the coop every time. Because of the way these dispensers are constructed, making adjustments can be as easy as purchasing some additional sections of PVC. Just adjust the height and lengths of the PVC pipes to fit your situation and needs. There are no magic lengths, although longer pipes will hold more feed and water, which is important if you have a large flock. The lengths shown here are just for illustrative purposes.

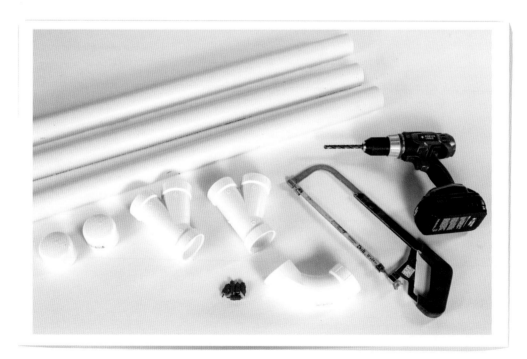

MATERIALS

Feeder Parts list:
- 4-foot (1¼-m) length 2-inch (5-cm) PVC pipe
- Two 2-inch (5-cm) PVC "Y" adapters
- Two 2-inch (5-cm) PVC end caps
- Assorted PVC fasteners/brackets to attach the feeder and waterer to your coop walls

Waterer Parts list:
- 2-inch (5-cm) PVC 90-degree "elbow" joint
- Two 5-foot (1½-m) lengths of 2-inch (5-cm) PVC pipe
- Five chicken waterer nipples (adjust number as needed)
- Tools needed:
- Pencil
- Hacksaw
- Chalk line
- Electric drill
- 11/32-inch (about 9-mm) drill bit
- 11-mm socket or nut driver (this was the size for the water nipples we used; yours may need a different size)

To build the feeder

Step 1: Modify PVC pipe

Start by making cuts to the 4-foot (1¼-m) PVC pipe. You'll need two 2-inch (5-cm) pieces of PVC for "spacers," so measure and cut these with the hacksaw. You'll also need to modify the remaining 44 inches (about 1¼ meters) of pipe to whatever length works for you and your coop; we shortened it to 38 inches (about 1 m).

Step 2: Build lower section

Assemble the lower section of the feeder (the part the chickens will actually eat out of). Combine a PVC end cap, a spacer, one PVC "Y" section, another spacer, and another "Y" section, as shown in the photos. You shouldn't need any glue or PVC cement; the pieces should all fit together snugly enough on their own.

Step 3: Build upper section

The upper section of the feeder acts as feed storage. Add the remaining long length of PVC pipe to the lower section you already built and then use another end cap for the top. You'll remove this end cap each time you want to fill the feeder.

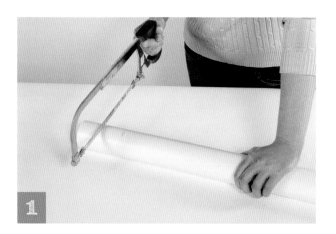
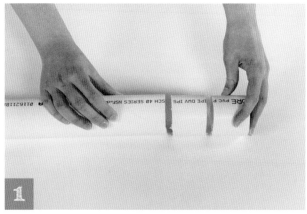
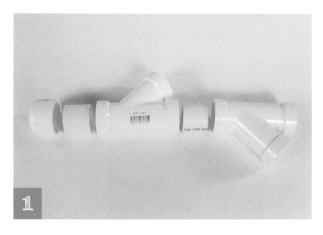
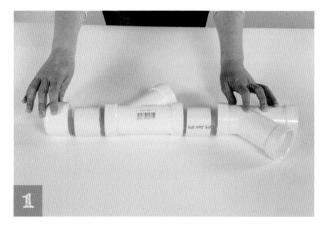

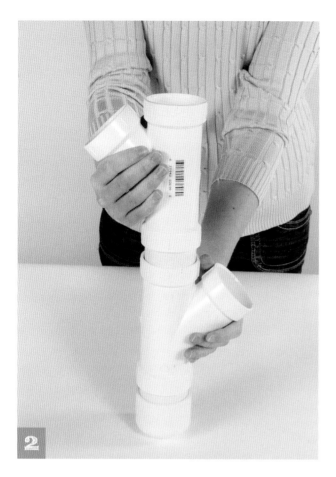

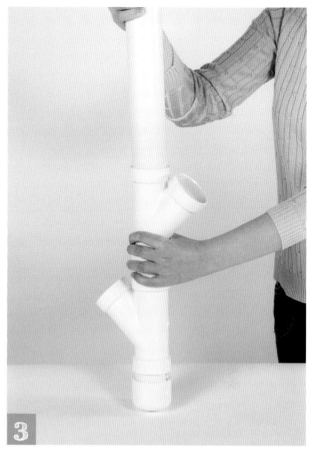

To build the waterer

Step 1: Mark holes

Mark a series of holes in one of the 5-foot (1½-m) PVC sections; these will be for the water nipples. The number of holes you choose depends on your flock, with approximately one nipple needed per one to three birds.

To prevent leakage or dripping, it's important that the water nipples hang vertically (not at an angle), so the holes need to be straight; you can use a carpenter's chalk line to help. Space the holes evenly; we went with 12 inches (30 cm) apart.

Step 2: Drill holes

Once you have marks, drill them out with whatever drill bit size is required for your water nipples; ours needed an $^{11}/_{32}$-inch (about 9-mm). PVC is tough and hard, and a little slippery, so take care when drilling into it. You might want to use a vise to help hold the pipes steady.

Step 3: Fasten water nipples

Follow the installation directions that come with your water nipples—some have a rubber seal built into them to prevent leakage, while others require a bit of thread sealing tape. Getting the nipples to thread into thick PVC can be a challenge. Once you've got them started, use a ratchet or a nut driver to tighten them all the way down.

Step 4: Add final elements

To finish, add an end cap and the 90-degree elbow joint to each end of the 5-foot (1½-m) PVC, then add the other 5-foot (1½-m) length of PVC to the elbow joint. This vertical PVC section is for the water storage, and, like the feeder, you can place another end cap on the top of it when you're not filling it.

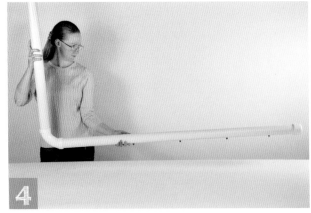

Additional Information

· You'll need some way to attach the feeders to your specific coop situation; this will vary depending on your setup, but purchasing a selection of PVC brackets/fasteners is probably a good starting point.

· The chickens should be naturally curious about the red color of the water nipples, and they may discover on their own that water comes out. If not, you may need to attempt to "demonstrate" how they work.

· Don't remove your chicken's current feed or water sources until you're positive they are using the new systems.

Compost Bin

Level of Difficulty: Intermediate
Length of Time: 2 hours

When you grow a garden in the same spot year after year, you'll soon learn what centuries of farmers and gardeners before you have learned: nutrients in the soil soon become depleted and need to be replaced. Happily, creating your own fertilizer via a compost bin is a simple, inexpensive way to keep your garden growing year after year—not to mention that it's an excellent way to freely dispose of organic kitchen scraps. And chicken keepers also have the opportunity to take advantage of this excellent—and free—fertilizer.

So why not make your own compost bin and get started? These instructions are for building a simple 3 x 3 x 3-foot (91 x 91 x 91-cm) compost bin, suitable for most household compost needs. If you're serious about creating compost for your garden, you can build three identical compost bins and always have compost in three stages: one that you're currently adding to, one that is in the process of composting, and one that is ready to use in the garden.

Lumber Type

Since your compost bin will be used outdoors, using treated lumber might seem like an obvious choice; however, this probably isn't the best idea because it's possible that some of the chemicals used for treatment could leach into your compost and end up in your garden. So use untreated lumber and simply realize that your compost bin's lifespan may be shortened as a result. One way to make the bin last longer is to use cedar lumber because cedar has natural properties that make it more water- and rot-resistant than other types of wood. One downside is that cedar is more expensive than other lumber, such as pine. You can use whatever your budget allows. We went for a compromise with our project, using untreated pine for the most of the bin but using cedar for the four bottom 2x4s (38 x 89 mm)-the ones that will actually be touching the ground and therefore most susceptible to rot.

MATERIALS

Cut list:

- 36 x 36-inch (91 x 91 cm) piece ½-inch (13-mm) plywood
- Four 36-inch (91-cm) 2x4s (38 x 89 mm)
- Two 33-inch (84-cm) 2x4s (38 x 89 mm)
- Two 32 3/4-inch (83-cm) 2x4s (38 x 89 mm)
- Twelve 29-inch (74-cm) 2x4s (38 x 89 mm)
- Two 28⅞-inch (73-cm) 2x4s (38 x 89 mm)
- Three 26-inch (66-cm) 2x4s (38 x 89 mm)
- Three 25¾-inch (65 cm) 2x4s (38 x 89 mm)
- 13 x 1½-inch (33 x 4-cm) piece ¾-inch (2-cm) pine or plywood

Parts list:

- Wood glue
- 6-inch (15-cm) screws
- 3½-inch (9-cm) screws
- 1¼-inch (3 cm) screws
- 1-inch (2½-cm) nails
- Roofing nails
- Two 6-inch (15-cm) hinges (for front panel)
- Two 2-inch (5-cm) hinges (for top access door)
- Two hook-and-eye latches
- Extra eye for access door handle
- Four 32 x 35-inch (81 x 89-cm) sections ¼-inch (6-mm) or ½-inch (13-mm) hardware cloth

Tools needed:

- Circular saw (a chop saw or radial arm saw can also be used to speed up the work)
- Jigsaw
- Wire snippers
- Hammer
- Screwdriver
- Electric drill
- Tape measure
- Framing square

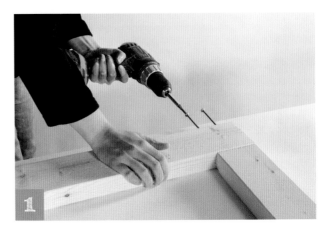

Step 1: Build four sides, part 1

The basic design for the four sides of the compost bin is the same, but there are small differences in measurements. In each case, begin by building a square, as shown in the photos. For the back panel, use two 33-inch (84-cm) 2x4s (38 x 89 mm) to create the top and bottom and two 29-inch (74-cm) 2x4s (38 x 89 mm) for the sides.

Since the front panel will function as a door that needs to swing, its measurements are slightly smaller than the back panel. Use two 32¾-inch (83-cm) 2x4s (38 x 89 mm)

Size

The smallest size you'll want to use for a compost bin is 3 x 3 x 3 feet (91 x 91 x 91 cm) as shown in this project; if you go smaller, the necessary fermenting action won't be as effective. You can, however, go larger than this if you have a large supply of composting materials. Fortunately, you could enlarge this basic design to other sizes.

for the top and bottom, and two 28⅞-inch (73-cm) 2x4s (38 x 89 mm) for the sides. The two side panels are identical: use two of the 36-inch (91-cm) 2x4s (38 x 89 mm) for the top and bottom, and two 29-inch (74-cm) 2x4s (38 x 89 mm) for the sides.

Use wood glue to strengthen the joints and then use 6-inch (15-cm) screws to secure. Use a framing square throughout the process to ensure that your joints stay square.

Step 2: Build four sides, part 2

Next, add three dividers to the interior of each square. For the back panel, use three 26-inch (66-cm) 2x4s (38 x 89 mm). For the front panel, use three 25¾-inch (65 cm) 2x4s (38 x 89 mm). For the side panels, use three 29-inch (74-cm) 2x4s (38 x 89 mm).

To achieve proper divider spacing, place each of them 4⅝ inches (12 cm) apart. Use 6-inch (15-cm) screws to secure.

Step 3: Attach hardware cloth

Using wire snippers, carefully cut four 32 x 35-inch (81 x 89-cm) sections of hardware cloth (we used hardware cloth with ¼-inch [6-mm] openings). Use roofing nails to fasten each 32 x 35-inch (81 x 89-cm) piece of hardware cloth to each of the four panels of the compost bin. This will allow plenty of airflow while still keeping the compost contained and reducing the chances of rodents or other animals entering the bin.

Safety Note

The cut edges of hardware cloth are super-sharp, so take care when working with and around it; at a minimum, wear safety glasses and gloves.

Step 4: Combine back and side panels

Start to assemble the compost bin. Using 3½-inch (9-cm) screws, attach the back panel to the two side panels. As shown in the photos, the back panel sits "inside" the two side panels. Again, using a framing square will help keep everything straight. When you're finished with this step, you'll have built a "U"-shape.

Step 5: Attach front panel

Now we'll add the front panel, which will act as a door. Using two 6-inch (15-cm) hinges along with 1¼-inch (3-cm) screws, attach the front panel to one of the side panels. (Since the front panel is slightly smaller than the others, you should have a little bit of "play" to help make the door swing.) Then use a small wood drill bit and power drill to make pilot holes for the two hook-and-eye latches. Screw in these latches in two locations to keep your front panel door shut.

Depending on where you plan to use your compost bin (rough ground, even ground), you may need to trim (rip) a small amount off of the front panel's bottom 32¾-inch (83-cm) 2x4 (38 x 89 mm) to help it swing and make sure it doesn't dig into the ground. Don't trim off too much, however, or you may invite rodents.

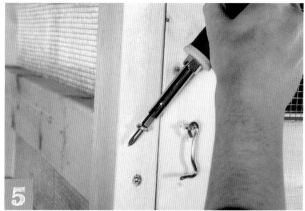

Step 6: Build top

Now you need to make some modifications to the 36 x 36-inch (91 x 91-cm) piece of plywood that will be used as the top, or "roof," of the compost bin. To provide an easy means for adding small amounts of material to the compost bin (coffee grinds, table scraps, and so on), we'll need to cut a small door. You can make the door any size you'd like; for our bin, we went with a 12 x 12-inch (30 x 30-cm) opening. Use a circular saw to do most of the work and a jigsaw to nicely finish the corners.

Next, attach a small doorstop on the underside of this hole. Use a piece of pine or plywood about 13 x 1½ inches (33 x 4 cm) and ¾ inch (2 cm) thick (this could be a scrap piece from another project, as the

Protection from Weather

Find a way to protect the plywood top of your compost bin from the elements. We used part of a simple vinyl outdoor tablecloth along with stretchable cord as a way to keep excessive moisture off the top of the compost bin.

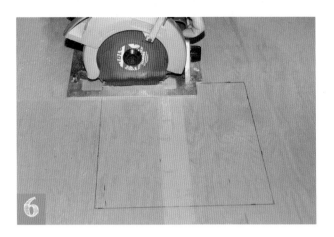

exact dimensions really don't matter much) and attach it with 1-inch (2½-cm) nails. Then attach the access door itself with two 2-inch (5-cm) hinges. Fasten the hinges with screws, but be sure to predrill the holes for best results. Then add a small handle (we used an extra eye from a hook-and-eye latch). Finally, place the 36 x 36-inch (91 x 91-cm) plywood on the top of the bin and secure with 1¼-inch (3-cm) screws.

Egg Incubator

Level of Difficulty: Advanced
Length of Time: 3 hours

Hatching chicks in an incubator—how fun! This can be an educational (and memorable) project to do with your kids or on your own. Maybe your flock is producing fertile eggs, or maybe you'd like to experiment with shipping in some fertile eggs from a hatchery that offers a specific breed you're interested in. Whatever the case, if you're going to hatch eggs in your home, you need an incubator. Store-bought incubators offer convenience and additional features, but building your own homemade incubator is a project that you can "DIY" and still expect suitable results.

The directions that follow are for building one example of a homemade incubator; there are many variations that can be just as successful. Some people build egg incubators out of old refrigerators; some try plastic or rubber storage totes. So feel free to modify these ideas to incorporate the parts you already have or can easily obtain.

The exact size of your Styrofoam cooler may differ from ours, and therefore you'd need to modify the dimensions of the plywood case. You might also opt to make your incubator a bit simpler or more complex; for instance, adding a fan or an additional lightbulb as a backup in case one burns out.

In any case, your goal is to maintain an incubator temperature of 97–101° F (36–38° C) at all times. Here, we're building a simple still-air incubator, meaning it doesn't have a fan to circulate the air (an incubator with a fan is called a forced-air incubator.) Because of this, you should probably aim for a slightly higher temperature of 101° F (38° C). Your eggs require a humidity of 50–55 percent for the first eighteen days, and upward of 65 percent for last three days. Don't let your incubator get too dry, or your eggs may not hatch. To control the humidity (such as to increase it for the last three days), simply experiment and adjust the amount of water in the baking pan. If you're not getting enough humidity, you can try adding a sponge to the pan; this should help bring more moisture into the environment.

For the first eighteen days, you must your eggs over two or three times each day. To help keep things clear, use a pencil to mark an X on one side and an O on the other (or some other marking system) to help you remember which side is which. During the last three days, you should not disturb your eggs at all—no turning.

MATERIALS

Cut list (modify if needed to fit your Styrofoam cooler):
- Two 11 x 16½-inch (28 x 42-cm) pieces ½-inch (13-mm)-thick plywood (for outer case short sides)
- Two 11 x 27¼-inch (28 x 69-cm) pieces ½-inch (13-mm)-thick plywood (for outer case long sides)
- 16½ x 26¼-inch (42 x 67-cm) piece ½-inch (13-mm)-thick plywood (for outer case base)

Parts list:
- Styrofoam cooler (ours was 25½ x 13 x 16 inches [65 x 33 x 41 cm])
- Plastic light fixture and two ½-inch (13 mm) screws
- Light fixture housing box and two ⅝-inch (16-mm) screws
- Electric power cord (grounded is helpful)
- 40-watt lightbulb
- "Lower" electric water-heater thermostat switch
- Digital thermometer/hydrometer
- 5 x 7-inch (13 x 18-cm) piece of glass or plastic (from a picture frame)
- 8 x 12-inch (20 x 30-cm) disposable aluminum baking pan
- Cooling rack
- Small towel
- Wood glue
- 1-inch (2½-cm) nails

Tools needed:
- Hammer
- Screwdriver
- Knife
- Utility knife
- Tape measure
- Electric drill
- Wire snippers
- Pliers

Step 1: Build wooden outer box

The Styrofoam cooler is used to insulate the eggs and keep the heat from the lightbulb from escaping. We chose to build an outer case from ½-inch (13-mm) plywood to protect the Styrofoam. Using wood glue and 1-inch (2½-cm) nails, create a five-sided box (leaving the top open). First, use the 16½ x 26¼-inch (42 x 67-cm) piece of plywood as a base. Next, add the two 11 x 16½-inch (28 x 42-cm) plywood pieces to create the short sides. Finally, use the two 11 x 27¼-inch (28 x 69-cm) pieces to add the long sides. Again, these dimensions fit our cooler (and are designed to leave a little wiggle room); you may have to make modifications to fit yours.

Step 2: Modify Styrofoam cooler

Next, we'll begin the slightly messy job of making some cuts to the cooler. On the back of the cooler, toward one side (as shown), score the rough shape of the light-fixture housing box. Then carefully cut this shape out of the Styrofoam. Keep a vacuum cleaner handy! Next, insert the fixture box into its hole. You'll also need to drill a ¾-inch (19-mm) hole in the wooden case right behind the box to allow for the electrical cord. Once that is complete, screw the housing box to the plywood case with ⅝-inch (16-mm) screws.

Additional Information

These directions are for a still-air (no fan) incubator, but you can modify the plan to add a fan for air circulation. Many people have success recycling a simple used 12-volt cooling fan from an old computer. If you decide to go this route, you'll need a 12-volt DC converter.

The water-heater thermostat is great because it constantly measures the ambient air temperature and automatically turns on or shuts off the lightbulb as needed to maintain the target temperature (which is adjustable with the switch). Some people who build homemade incubators swap the thermostat for a dimmer switch and control the temperature by brightening or dimming the light, but this requires more attention and fine-tuning to maintain ideal warmth, while the water-heater thermostat does this for you. If you find your thermostat is allowing too much of a temperature variation, you can experiment with increasing or decreasing its distance from the lightbulb.

As with all things electrical, safety is of primary concern when building and using your incubator. Take care when wiring and don't plug anything in until you're done working and sure that everything is correct. If you're unsure about any of the wiring or electrical procedures, be sure to get help from someone knowledgeable.

Take care to keep the incubator in a place where it won't be disturbed or knocked over—not only must you keep the eggs safe, but you also don't want the water source to spill near or on the electrical parts.

Understand that incubating eggs properly is challenging, and 100-percent success is not always possible. Even slight shifts in temperature or humidity can be enough to cause some eggs to fail, so be prepared for that ahead of time.

Step 3: Cut window

A glass window on the top of the incubator is very handy for allowing you to monitor the temperature, humidity, and eggs without opening the lid. Again, score the outline of the 5 x 7-inch (13 x 18-cm) piece of glass and then cut out the Styrofoam slightly to the inside (¼ inch [6 mm]), so that the hole is a bit too small. Next, cut a small "shelf" for the glass to sit on, so that when you're all finished, the glass sits flush with the cooler lid. Use some clear tape to smoothly attach the edges of the glass in place.

Step 4: Prepare ventilation

The chicks inside the eggs need air to breathe—they can breathe right through their eggshells—so it's important to add some ventilation to your incubator. Using a drill and a ½-inch (13-mm) wood bit, carefully drill a series of ½-inch (13-mm) holes into the Styrofoam. There are no hard and fast rules, so this is another aspect you can experiment with; you might opt to add more holes (and even add holes through the wooden outer case), or, if you think your incubator is getting too much of a draft, you can re-cover some of the ventilation holes with tape.

Step 5: Begin wiring

Now we'll start to do some simple wiring for the light fixture and thermostat switch. Using a razor knife, strip away about 8 inches (20 cm) of the outer casing of the grounded electrical cord. Snip off the ground (green) wire; we'll use that in a minute. Feed the black and white wires through the hole in the fixture box. Leave black in the middle, but feed the white wire off through the side.

Step 6: Install thermostat switch

Attach the thermostat switch to the cooler wall, somewhere near the lightbulb (we screwed right into the Styrofoam; you could also use tape or glue). Attach the white wire to one of the thermostat screws and then use that leftover piece of ground wire to connect the other screw back to the fixture box as shown (if you aren't using a grounded cord, just use any few inches of electrical wire you have handy).

Step 7: Wire light fixture

Attach the black wire to the brass screw on the light fixture and the other wire to the silver. Screw the light fixture into the housing box and insert a 40-watt lightbulb (your heat source).

Step 8: Add water source

We'll need a simple water source to add humidity to the incubator. A disposable aluminum baking pan works great, although you can use just about anything that will hold water. We also need somewhere to place our eggs; an elevated cooling rack worked great for our setup. (To keep the eggs from rolling around, you can place them on a small towel.) Add in your thermometer/hydrometer.

Step 9: Test before using

Turn on your incubator and monitor your setup for a day or two prior to adding eggs to make sure that you have the temperature and humidity correct as well as to give you time to make any necessary adjustments. When you're satisfied that everything is good to go, put in your eggs.

Nest Boxes

Level of Difficulty: Advanced
Length of Time: 3 hours

Your chickens don't necessarily need help in order to be happy layers. They'll lay their eggs just about anywhere if you let them, but that can be a problem. Nobody likes cracked or dirty eggs, and that's what might happen if your hens are allowed to select any nesting place they desire. Instead, it's best to casually suggest a more desirable place for your hens to lay their eggs—somewhere that will be safe, clean, and comfortable for the hens to use and easy for you to access. Happily, there is such a place, and you can build it. We're talking, of course, about a nest box.

Although it may seem surprising, every hen does not require her own nest box. In fact, sometimes multiple hens try to use the same one. Generally, you'll want to provide one nest box for every two to four hens. Ideally, each nest box will provide around 1 cubic foot (30 x 30 x 30 cm) of space, although it's nice to add a little more height (12 to 14 inches [30 to 36 cm]).

The unit we're going to build here contains three nest boxes, which is enough for six to twelve hens to happily lay their eggs. It also has a slanted roof, which is ideal for nest boxes because it discourages the birds from sitting on the nest box roof and making a considerable mess. These nest boxes are lightweight and easy to move. The only tools you'll need are a hammer and a circular saw, although a table saw would make some of the cuts easier.

Nest Pads

One of the important purposes of a nest box is to aid in keeping your eggs clean. You can go one step further in your quest for clean eggs by using chicken nest pads in your nest box. Rather than just using ordinary chicken bedding in the nest box, a nest pad is a one-piece bedding layer designed to be comfortable for your hens, easy to clean, and removable. Chicken nest pads are specially designed to prevent the buildup of chicken manure and to keep the eggs slightly elevated, out of any mess.

MATERIALS

Cut list:
- Four 14 x 18¼-inch (36 x 46-cm) pieces ½-inch (13-mm)-thick plywood (for side walls and dividers)
- 35 x 3-inch (89 x 8-cm) piece ½-inch (13-mm)-thick plywood (for front trim)
- 35 x 18¼-inch (89 x 46-cm) piece ½-inch (13-mm)-thick plywood (for back wall)
- 35 x 15¾-inch (89 x 40-cm) piece ½-inch (13-mm)-thick plywood (for roof)

Parts list:
- 1½-inch (4-cm) nails
- Wood glue

Tools needed:
- Hammer
- Electric drill
- Circular saw or table saw
- Pin nailer (optional)

Step 1: Prepare sides and dividers

Start off by modifying the four 14 x 18¼-inch (36 x 46-cm) pieces of plywood, using either a circular saw or table saw. These will become the sides and dividers of the nest boxes, and each one needs a diagonal cut to create the slanted roof. Make a straight cut from a point 13 inches (33 cm) up one of the long sides to the top of opposite corner, as shown in the photos. Do this for all four pieces.

Step 2: Fasten dividers

Next, fasten the back wall to the four side/divider panels. Using wood glue and nails (it's a good idea to predrill your holes), use two of the modified 14 x 18¼-inch (36 x 46-cm) pieces to create the side walls and the other two to create the internal dividers. You can use an air pin nailer, or you can predrill holes and use a hammer.

Step 3: Add front trim

Put the 35 x 3-inch (89 x 8-cm) piece in place to create the front trim; this gives each nest box a complete perimeter and keeps eggs from rolling out.

Step 4: Install roof

Glue and nail the 35 x 15¾-inch (89 x 40-cm) roof into place.

Egg Candler

Level of Difficulty: Intermediate

Length of Time: 2 hours

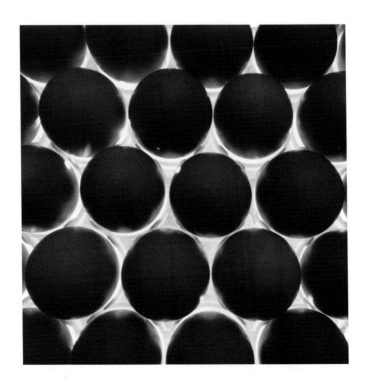

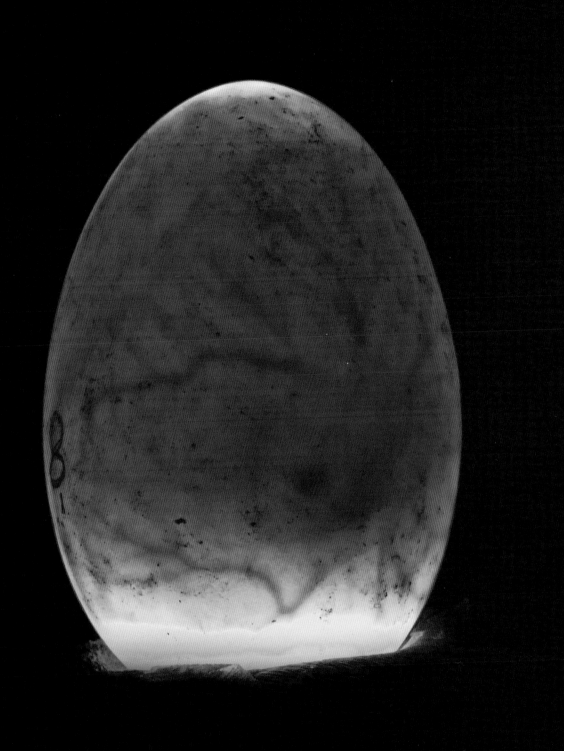

Farmers have been "candling" eggs for hundreds of years. It's a simple process that involves shining a light through an unhatched egg to illuminate the interior and monitor chick development and egg viability. Historically, and as the name suggests, actual candles were used as the light source, but this process is difficult due to the dim light and the flickering of the candle, not to mention its heat.

When incubating eggs, you'll need to keep an eye on them to observe which ones are developing properly, which are not developing, and which were never fertilized. Candling is the way to do this. Happily, you can build your own candler with just a few simple parts and—best of all—a standard lightbulb in place of a candle.

You can take several different approaches when building an egg candler. It's a simple item that can be as plain or fancy as you'd like. It's possible to recycle a large, empty coffee can (or similar item) by placing your lightbulb inside and cutting a hole in the bottom of the can (which then becomes the top). Alternatively, you can opt to utilize the reflector from an old clamp light by inverting it and using it to hold your egg while directing light through it. For this project, we're going to create a slightly more attractive—but still very simple—wooden version. The advantage is that you will have a more substantial and permanent tool that will last longer and stand up to more use. We spruced up our finished product by decorating it with a photograph of a chick. You can do the same, or you might opt to paint, stencil, or stain your egg candler.

A couple of notes: As with all things electrical, safety is of primary concern. Egg candlers may be inclined to overheat due to the close confines of the bulb and the box. Never leave your egg candler unattended because heat will develop when the candler is in use. Don't leave an egg on the candler for more than the time it takes to observe it. Additionally (for the electrically inclined), you can add an on/off switch to the light or, to keep things simple, just connect it to a power strip with a switch. Turn the candler off between eggs, keeping it cool and safe. Unplug the candler when it's not in use.

MATERIALS

Cut list:
- Six 6 x 7-inch (15 x 18-cm) pieces ½-inch (13-mm)-thick plywood
- Two 1¼ x 3-inch (3 x 8-cm) pieces of ½-inch (13-mm)-thick plywood

Parts list:
- Porcelain light fixture and two 1-inch (2½-cm) screws
- Electrical power cord
- 75-watt bulb or fluorescent bulb
- 1-inch (2½-cm) nails
- Wood glue
- Power strip
- Wire staple (optional)

Tools needed:
- Electric drill
- Hammer
- Screwdriver

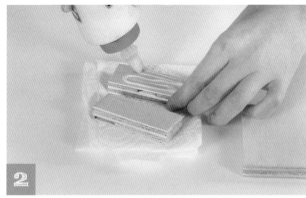

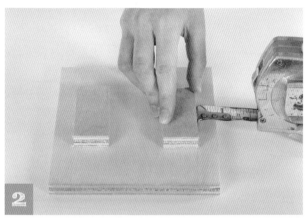

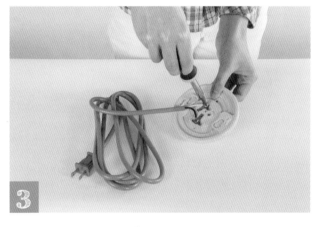

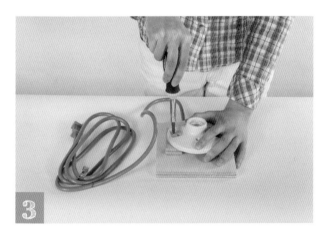

Step 1: Modify plywood

Drill a 1-inch (2½-cm) hole in the center of one piece of 6 x 7-inch (15 x 18-cm) plywood. Cut a ½ x ½ x ½-inch (13 mm x 13 mm x 13-mm) notch in the bottom of one of the other pieces. Set these pieces aside until Step 5.

Step 2: Prepare base

Build the base first because the base is where you will fasten the light fixture. Glue the two 1¼ x 3-inch (3 x 8-cm) pieces of plywood to one of the 6 x 7-inch (15 x 18-cm) pieces of plywood (place them about ¾ inch [19 mm] in). These two blocks will give you a place to screw down the porcelain light fixture.

Step 3: Install cord

Next, attach the electrical cord to the light fixture, following the directions included with the cord or fixture (black goes to the brass screw, white to the silver).

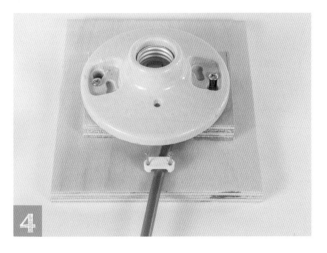

Step 4: Attach fixture

Once the cord is attached, carefully screw the light fixture to the base using 1-inch (2½-cm) screws (probably provided with the light fixture). Predrill your holes to keep life easy. Alternatively, you can use a wire staple to pin the cord to the center. Screw in the bulb and test it to make sure everything is working. Set aside your finished base.

Step 5: Build candling box

Use the five remaining 6 x 7-inch (15 x 18-cm) pieces of plywood to create a five-sided box (it will fit over the base and remain separate to allow you to access the light bulb). Glue and fasten with 1-inch (2 ½-cm) nails; again, predrill the nail holes for best results. Use the piece with the 1-inch (2 ½-cm) hole as the top, and use the piece with the ½-inch (13-mm) notch as the back, with the notch positioned down at the open end of the box.

Step 6: Add reflector

If you'd like your egg candler to be a little brighter, you can line the interior of the box with aluminum foil to act as a reflector and bounce more of the light out through the hole.

Step 7: Use in the dark

Candle your eggs in a dark room for best visibility.

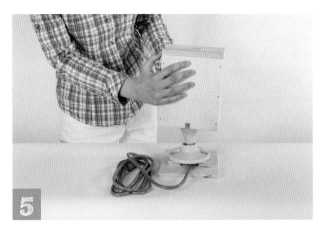

Chicken Roost

Level of Difficulty: Intermediate
Length of Time: 3 hours

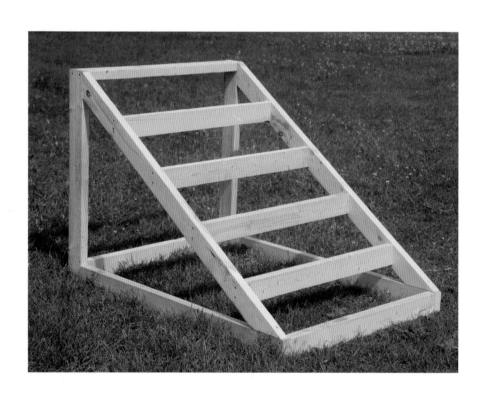

Chickens don't actually sleep in their nest boxes; nest boxes are (and should!) be used only for laying. Instead, when dusk falls, chickens have a natural desire to get up in the air, away from the ground. The reason for this is simple: a drowsy chicken is a prime target for nocturnal predators like foxes, skunks, raccoons, and others. Even though your chickens may have always lived in a coop and are the product of years of domestication, chickens retain a natural instinct to get up off the ground at night and find a safe and elevated place to rest. You can provide for this need in your coop by building your chickens a roost.

But do your chickens still need a roost even if predators can't get inside the coop? Absolutely. Besides providing for the chickens' "psychological" need to roost—which is important in its own right—offering a roost promotes better health by keeping the chickens away from some of the bacteria that can develop on the floor of the coop. Roosts will also encourage hens to avoid sleeping in a nest box, which can lead to unsanitary laying conditions.

It's also important to have enough roosts for your entire flock. This is because of the flock's hierarchy: birds at the top of the hierarchy will have first access to the best (that is, the highest) roost positions, while chickens that are lower in the pecking order will be left with the lower roosts. And if there isn't enough room, some birds will be left with nowhere to roost. So take this into consideration when planning your roost system.

There are multiple ways to approach the roost situation. You could build a stand-alone unit suitable for a large, walk-in-type coop, or you could create a series of "built-in" roosts for the chickens. Some people build elaborate roosts while others opt for a rustic look and use actual tree branches (with bark) to get the job done. For this project, we'll show you how to make a larger stand-alone roost with room to support quite a few chickens.

The particular roost we describe here is somewhat large and may not fit through the door of your coop, so measure your doorway before building. If your door isn't wide enough, you can assemble the roost *inside* the coop (make your cuts somewhere else, though), or you can adjust the width of the roost to make sure it fits through your doorway.

Note: Pine will work fine for indoor use.

MATERIALS

Cut list:
- Two 5-foot (1½-m) 2x4s (38 x 89 mm)
- Two 4-foot (1¼-m) 2x4s (38 x 89 mm)
- Nine 3-foot (91-cm) 2x4s (38 x 89 mm)

Parts list:
- Box of 3½-inch (9-cm) screws
- Box of 6-inch (15-cm) screws

Tools needed:
- Electric drill
- Framing square
- Level
- Miter saw

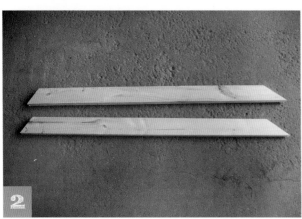

Step 1: Assemble side panels, part 1

The basic frame of the roost is designed around two identical triangles. To begin, use 6-inch (15-cm) screws to fasten one of the 4-foot (1¼-m) 2x4s (38 x 89 mm) to a 3-foot (91-cm) 2x4 (38 x 89 mm) at a right angle (the 3-foot [91-cm] 2x4 [38 x 89 mm] should be "on the ground"—not sitting on top of the 4-foot [1¼-m] 2x4 [38 x 89 mm]). As always, the framing square can help you keep everything straight.

Step 2: Assemble side panels, part 2

Cut two angles on each end of the 5-foot (1½-m) 2x4 (38 x 89 mm). Have someone help you hold the 5-foot (1½-m) 2x4 (38 x 89 mm) in place so that you can "score" the necessary angles with a pencil and then cut the two angles. You can then use 6-inch (15-cm) screws to fasten the (now-modified) 5-foot (1½-m) 2x4 (38 x 89 mm) on top to complete the triangle. Repeat steps 1 and 2 to build the second triangle.

Step 3: Combine side panels

Now take two 3-foot (91-cm) 2x4s (38 x 89 mm) and use 3½-inch (9-cm) screws to fasten them to the front and back of the roost (as shown) to create the lower base. The structure should now be able to stand up on its own while you finish working.

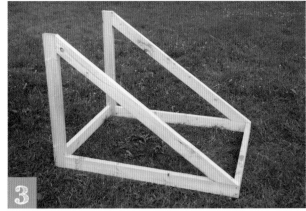

Step 4: Add roosts

Now use the final four 3-foot (91-cm) 2x4s (38 x 89 mm) and 3½-inch (9-cm) screws to add the actual roosting places in a stair-step pattern about 12 inches (30 cm) apart. Position the roosts "vertically" so that the birds will be roosting on the narrow edge of the wood. A level can be helpful to keep the roosts straight.

Optional: Rounded roosts

It's easy to add rounded perches for your chickens. For this modification, we used round wooden handrails (about 2 x 2 inches [5 x 5 cm]) cut to 3 feet (91-cm) and screwed them onto the top of each roost. This provides the chickens with a slightly more comfortable perch.

Dropping Board

Level of Difficulty: Beginner

Length of Time: 1 hour

After your chickens have used a roost for some time, you'll notice that one drawback is the mess that can accumulate directly underneath. If you'd like to make things easier on clean-out days, you can utilize a dropping board.

This is a very simple project that you can—and should—modify to the specific dimensions of your coop. Some folks go the disposable dropping-board route, which means hanging or placing a section of tarp or plastic under the roost and then throwing it out and exchanging it for another as needed. This is a viable option, but this project will show you how to add a basic wooden dropping board to the stand-alone roost (see page 88) that you can install, remove, and replace easily. Cleaning the wooden dropping board should be a fairly straightforward process, but if it becomes overly soiled, you can replace it with minimal cost and effort.

Note: The dimensions of this dropping board will fit the roost described on page 88. If you modified the size of the roost, modify the size of the dropping board accordingly.

MATERIALS

Cut list:
- 51 x 35½-inch (1¼ m x 90-cm) piece of ½-inch (13-mm)-thick plywood
- Two 24-inch (61-cm) 2x4s (38 x 89 mm)

Parts list:
- 5-inch (13-cm) handle
- Two ½-inch (13-mm) screws
- Box of 3½-inch (9-cm) screws

Tools needed:
- Table saw
- Circular saw
- Electric drill
- Screwdriver
- Tape measure

Step 1: Construct plywood base

Cut your plywood to 51 x 35½ inches (1¼ m x 90 cm). Large pieces of plywood like this can be difficult to cut, so it's ideal if you use a table saw for this job because it's the most precise—and easiest—method for making long rips. Alternatively, a circular saw can do the job, but it will be more tiring and less accurate.

Step 2: Attach 2x4s

To give the dropping-board plywood a place to rest, use the two 24-inch (61-cm) 2x4s (38 x 89 mm) to create "runners" along the inside of the roost unit; we placed these 6 inches (15 cm) in from the back of the roost. You could also make the runners the entire length of the roost, but this isn't required, and using shorter lumber pieces gives you a chance to use up some scraps. Using 3½-inch (9-cm) screws should be just right.

Step 3: Add handle

Use a tape measure to center a small screen-door handle (we used a 5-inch [13-cm] handle) on the front end of the plywood and use two short screws (less than the thickness of the plywood) to hold it in place. Be careful not to allow these screws to poke through to the bottom.

Chick Brooder

Level of Difficulty: Intermediate

Length of Time: 2 hours

Whether you've hatched chicks from an incubator or had them delivered, one fact is clear: they will need a safe, warm place to live until they are large enough to be allowed into the main coop with the rest of the flock. The solution is to place the chicks in a simple box known as a *brooder* while they grow, develop feathers, and become more self-reliant. You can make your own brooder out of simple materials, and it can be as basic or as elaborate as you'd like. For this project, we're constructing a brooder made out of a clear plastic storage tote, an item that is readily available and easy to modify. The design of this brooder is based on the size of the plastic storage tote we had on hand, but you can easily make any needed modifications if your brooder box is a different size.

There are several key criteria to meet when raising chicks in a brooder, including the following:

Temperature. For newly hatched chicks, the temperature in the brooder should initially start out at 95°F (35°C), but it needs to decrease by 5 degrees F (2¾ degrees C) every week as the chicks grow and develop feathers. Generally, you adjust the temperature by raising the lamp higher and farther away from the brooder, but you could also control the heat by means of a dimmer switch. In any case, it's critical to keep a thermometer inside the brooder to allow you to monitor the temperature. Also, pay attention to the behavior of your chicks. If they're crowded together under the light, they may be too cold; likewise, if they're spread out and seem to be avoiding the area directly under the light, the brooder may be too hot.

Cleanliness. It is critical for the bedding to stay dry and clean to prevent a buildup of moisture and bacteria that could cause illness to the still-vulnerable chicks. A few inches of pine shavings can work just fine, but don't use cedar shavings because they are not safe for chicks.

Size. Don't overcrowd the brooder; you can always make another one or use a box with larger dimensions if you're raising a large number of chicks.

MATERIALS

Cut list:
- Two 1 x 14-inch (2½ x 36-cm) strips of ½-inch (13-mm)-thick plywood
- Two 1 x 11½-inch (2½ x29-cm) strips of ½-inch (13-mm)-thick plywood
- 10½ x 15-inch (27 x 38-cm) section of ½-inch (13-mm) hardware cloth

Parts needed:
- 23½ x 16⅛ x 12¼-inch (34 x 41 x 31-cm) clear plastic storage tote with lid
- Brooder heat lamp with bulb
- Simple thermometer
- Chick waterer
- Chick feeder
- Ten 1-inch (2½-cm) bolts with nuts
- Bag of pine bedding

Tools needed:
- Utility knife
- Tape measure
- Wire snippers
- Pliers
- Screwdriver
- Electric drill
- Ruler or framing square
- Pencil

Step 1: Measure and cut lid

Begin by making modifications to the lid of the brooder. For the dimensions of our storage tote, a hole of 9½ x 14 inches (24 x 36 cm) was just about right. Leave a couple of spare inches free on each side of the hole to avoid interfering with the locking mechanism and structural components of the lid. Use a ruler (or framing square) and pencil to mark straight lines for your cuts and then carefully use a utility knife to remove the plastic.

Step 2: Measure and cut hardware cloth

Use wire snippers to cut out a 10½ x 15-inch (27 x 38-cm) section of ½-inch (13-mm) hardware cloth. This spacing will allow plenty of airflow but still keeps the chicks protected. Wear gloves and eye protection when handling the hardware cloth. Once you've cut the hardware cloth, set it aside momentarily.

Step 3: Drill holes

Next, use the strips of ½-inch (13-mm) plywood to create a frame around the hole in the plastic lid as shown in the photos. Once the frame is in position, use the electric drill to drill several holes in the plywood strips and all the way through the plastic underneath. Use a drill bit with a diameter that is just slightly larger than the diameter of the bolts (for us, this was a ⁹⁄₁₆-inch (14-mm) bit).

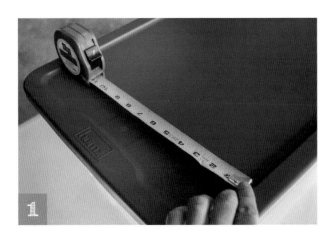

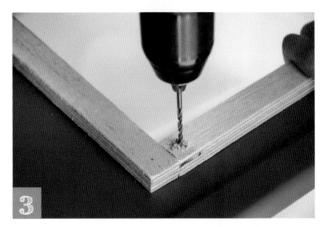

Step 4: Add bolts

With the holes prepared in the plywood and plastic, put the hardware cloth back in place under the plywood. Use the ten 1-inch (2½-cm) bolts and nuts to secure the hardware cloth in place. Use pliers and a screwdriver to tighten the bolts.

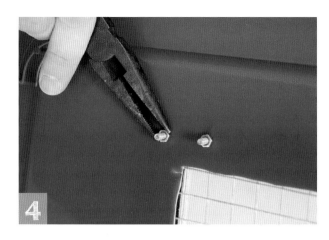

Step 5: Add accessories

Add a few inches of bedding to the brooder, along with a feeder and waterer for the chicks and a basic thermometer, which will allow you to monitor the temperature in the coop.

Step 6: Mount lamp and test temperature

Test out the brooder before using. Mount the heat lamp nearby, pointed at the hole in the lid of the brooder, and observe the thermometer until you reach the desired temperature (initially 95°F [35°C]). You will likely need to adjust the heat lamp's wattage/distance and experiment until you find the right combination to give you the proper temperature.

Quarantine Habitat

Level of Difficulty: Advanced
Length of Time: 4 hours

It's never a fun topic to think about, but whenever we take on the responsibility of caring for animals, there is always the possibility that one could become sick. Chickens are no exception. There's also the possibility that the illness could be contagious and spread to other members of the flock. To help prevent this from happening, monitor the flock's health each day and immediately remove any chicken that begins to show signs of illness.

Ideally, you will have a completely separate location in which to house the sick chicken; if you simply confine the affected chicken to a separate area of the same coop, the chickens might still come into contact with one another and spread the disease. It's helpful to build a "sick pen" or "quarantine habitat" and set it aside so it's ready in case the need arises.

These instructions are for a fairly small habitat that is easy to build and could be used for one or two chickens. It's a fairly robust enclosure, but ideally you would use it inside another shelter of some sort (a barn or the like) because it isn't entirely predator-proof or weatherproof. The habitat isn't designed or intended for long-term use but as a means of quarantining and monitoring sick birds until they are well enough to rejoin the main flock.

The construction of this project will benefit greatly from a few additional tools. A table saw is the best tool for creating the 2 x 2-foot (61 x 61-cm) sections of plywood, although you could use a circular saw. The circular saw is harder to use and provides less accuracy, however. You will need a jigsaw for some of the notching and for the construction of the door, and a chop saw or miter saw will help speed up the process of cutting the multiple 2x4s (38 x 89 cm).

MATERIALS

Cut list:
- Four 3-foot (91-cm) 2x4s (38 x 89 cm)
- Four 21-inch (53-cm) 2x4s (38 x 89 cm)
- Four 17-inch (43-cm) 2x4s (38 x 89 cm)
- Three 2 x 2-foot (61 x 61-cm) sections of ½-inch (13-mm)-thick plywood
- Two 20½ x 20½ (52 x 52-cm) sections of ½-inch (13-mm) hardware cloth
- 22½ x 20½-inch (57 x 52-cm) section of ½-inch (13-mm) hardware cloth

Parts list:
- Box of 6-inch (15-cm) exterior screws
- Box of 3-inch (8-cm) exterior screws
- Box of 1-inch (2½-cm) exterior screws
- Two 2-inch (5-cm) hinges
- Hook-and-eye latch

Tools needed:
- Table saw
- Circular saw
- Jigsaw
- Miter or chop saw
- Electric drill
- Framing square
- Pencil
- Tape measure
- Wire snippers
- Staple gun and staples or hammer and roofing nails

Step 1: Assemble sides

Take two of the 3-foot (91-cm) 2x4s (38 x 89 cm) and use 6-inch (15-cm) screws to join them together with one 17-inch (43-cm) 2x4 (38 x 89 cm), arranged to create an "H" shape as shown in the photos. There should be a distance of 1 foot (30 cm) from the ground up to the bottom of the 17-inch (43-cm) 2x4 (38 x 89 cm). (The habitat will end up as a 2 x 2-foot [61 x 61-cm] cube on 1-foot [30-cm] legs.) Repeat to create two identical sides.

Step 2: Combine sides

Take two of the 21-inch (53-cm) 2x4s (38 x 89 cm) and use 3-inch (8-cm) screws to join the two sides together and create the four-legged basic frame of the habitat. These 21-inch (53-cm) 2x4s (38 x 89 cm) should also be 1 foot (30 cm) up from the ground. The structure will now stand freely on its own.

Step 3: Prepare floor

Next comes the floor of the habitat. Take one of the 2 x 2-foot (61 x 61-cm) pieces of plywood and, using a jigsaw, mark and cut out a 3½ x 1½-inch (9 x 4-cm) notch on each corner as shown in the photos. These notches will allow the plywood floor to slip down inside the frame of the habitat and rest on the 2x4s (38 x 89 cm). Use 1-inch (2½-cm) screws to fasten it down.

Step 4: Add upper frame and roof

Use two more 17-inch (43-cm) 2x4s (38 x 89 cm) and two more 21-inch (53-cm) 2x4s (38 x 89 cm) to create an upper frame for the habitat in the same manner as the lower 2x4s (38 x 89 cm). Use 3-inch (8-cm) and 6-inch (15-cm) screws, respectively. Next, use a 2 x 2-foot (61 x 61-cm) piece of plywood to make a roof. Use 1-inch (2½-cm) screws to secure it.

Step 5: Build door

Three sides of the habitat will be covered in hardware cloth, but one side of the habitat needs to be plywood to create a door and possibly provide shade. Begin by making some modifications to the remaining 2 x 2-foot (61 x 61-cm) piece of plywood to create a door. Using a pencil, mark out a 15 x 18-inch (38 x 46-cm) opening that is situated 3 inches (8 cm) in from each side, 3½ inches (9 cm) up from the bottom, and 5½ inches (14 cm) down from the top. Carefully use a circular saw to begin cutting out the door. A jigsaw can be helpful in the corners for extra precision.

Step 6: Attach door to frame

With the door cut out, use the 2-inch (5-cm) hinges and hook-and-eye latch to fasten the door to its frame. Place the hinges at the bottom so that the door swings down. Then, attach the entire section of plywood to the habitat with 1-inch (2½-cm) screws; put it on one of the ends that has the 21-inch (53-cm) 2x4s.

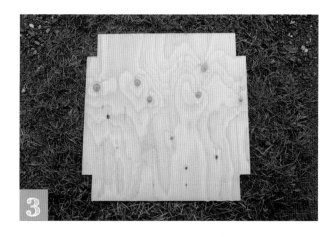

Step 7: Cut and attach hardware cloth

With wire snippers, carefully cut three sections of ½-inch (13-mm) hardware cloth: one 22½ x 20½ inches (57 x 52-cm) and two 20½ x 20½ inches (52 x 52-cm). Attach the hardware cloth to the habitat using staples or roofing nails: the single 22½ x 20½-inch (57 x 52-cm) piece goes opposite the door, on an end with 21-inch (53-cm) 2x4s (38 x 89 cm). The two 20½ x20½-inch (52 x 52-cm) pieces go on the sides with the 17-inch (43-cm) 2x4s (38 x 89 cm). Optional: Add a small amount of trim to cover the edges of the hardware cloth.

Collapsible Chicken Run

Level of Difficulty: Advanced
Length of Time: 3 hours

You might like to have the ability to allow your chickens to free-range for part of the day so that they can utilize new areas. But you may still want to contain your chickens in a specific area so that you can protect them from predators and control where they range.

There are a number of ways to create a portable chicken run, including the popular chicken tractor, but you can also make a simple and easy-to-build fold-up 4 x 4-foot (1¼ x 1¼-m) chicken run that collapses into a small, lightweight package whenever you want to move it or store it.

In these instructions, we'll show you one way to create a simple collapsible chicken run. You can certainly make variations to this design; for instance, you could opt for a larger 8 x 8-foot (2½ x 2½-m) run by essentially doubling the "recipe" given here.

MATERIALS

Cut list:
- Sixteen 24½-inch (62-cm) 1x2s (19 x 38-mm)
- Sixteen 23-inch (58-cm) 1x2s (19 x 38-mm)

Parts list:
- Eight 24 x 24-inch (61 x 61-cm) sections of ¼-inch (6-mm) or ½-inch (13-mm) hardware cloth
- Two hook-and-eye latches
- Fourteen 2-inch (5-cm) hinges
- Box of 1½-inch (4-cm) nails
- Box of staples
- Wood glue

Tools needed:
- Circular saw or miter saw
- Staple gun or hammer
- Electric drill or screwdriver
- Framing square
- Wire snippers

Step 1: Assemble panel frames

To begin, we'll assemble the actual frames that will form the skeleton of the collapsible chicken pen. We'll need eight complete frames. Take two of the 24½-inch (62-cm) 1x2s (19 x 38-mm) and two of the 23-inch (58-cm) 1x2s (19 x 38-mm) and use them to create a square, with the shorter 23-inch (58-cm) 1x2s (19 x 38-mm) on the "inside," and the longer 24½-inch (62-cm) 1x2s (19 x 38-mm) on the "outside," as shown in the photos. Use a framing square to help you achieve precise corners. Predrill nail holes with a small drill bit and then fasten with 1½-inch (4-cm) nails. Use wood glue on each joint for a firmer bond. Repeat this seven more times to create a total of eight wooden squares.

Step 2: Cut hardware cloth

Next, we'll add the hardware cloth to each panel. Using your choice of ¼-inch (6-mm) or ½-inch (13-mm) hardware cloth, carefully cut a total of eight 24 x 24-inch (61 x 61-cm) squares with wire snippers. (Our supplier provides hardware cloth on rolls 4 feet [1¼ m] wide, so it was a simple matter to purchase a 4 x 8-foot [1¼ x 2½-m] section to use for this project.)

Predator-Proofing Tips

· Half-inch (13-mm) hardware cloth may be available in a stronger gauge than ¼-inch (6-mm), which can help keep predators out. Don't use chicken wire for this project because predators can easily get past chicken wire. Hardware cloth is essential.

· If you'd like to create a roof for the collapsible run, make one 4 x 4-foot (1¼ x 1¼-m) frame and cover it with hardware cloth. Temporarily screw down the roof when the chickens are using the pen.

· You can use 2x2s (38 x 38 mm) or larger lumber instead of 1x2s (19 x 38 mm) for the basic frame; this will be make the run stronger, although it will also make the run heavier and more cumbersome to move and handle.

· Because this pen is lightweight and portable, it does not offer adequate protection against digging or large predators. Your chickens should be kept in a dig-proof coop at night. Only use this chicken run during the day in a place where you can keep an eye on the chickens.

· Using this pen inside a larger area protected by electric fencing may help keep predators away.

Step 3: Fasten hardware cloth

Attach the 24 x 24-inch (61 x 61-cm) sections of hardware cloth to each of the eight wooden panel frames. We used a manual staple gun, but you could also use roofing nails to pin down the hardware cloth. It's important to keep the edges straight and properly aligned with the wooden frame. It's also critical that you exercise extreme care when handling the wire (safety glasses and gloves are a must!).

Step 4: Attach hinges

We can begin to fasten the finished panels together to create the pen. This can be a tricky step because you must assemble the hinges and frames the right way to allow

the pen to expand and collapse properly. Use two 2-inch (5-cm) hinges on each joint, and screw them in with the electric drill or screwdriver (it can help to predrill the screw holes). Here's an easy way to make sure that the panels will assemble in the correct manner:

- Create four pairs of panels, each with the hardware cloth facing out.

- Place all four pairs (a total of eight panels) side by side.

- Attach hinges to each of the four pairs (shown in the photo).

- Go around to the other side

- Attach hinges to the six inner panels, leaving off the two panels on each end (shown in the photo).

Step 5: Add latches
Use two hook-and-eye latches at the top and bottom to secure the opening, and you're ready to use your pen.

Chicken Ramp

Level of Difficulty: Intermediate
Length of Time: 2 hours

Anytime your chickens need easy access to an elevated area, such as a coop door, you'll want to supply them with a chicken ramp (sometimes called a chicken ladder). A chicken ramp is merely an inclined plane with steps added to provide additional grip and allow the chickens to climb the ramp even when it's wet. The ramp we're going to build in this project is long enough to be useful in a variety of situations. Be careful to not make the ramp's angle to be too steep because this will make it difficult for the chickens to use. Making the ramp longer will allow chickens to reach higher areas while still avoiding steep angles.

These instructions are for a ramp that is 4 feet (1¼ m) long. Because of the project's simplicity, you can easily modify the ramp to suit your particular needs. Keep in mind that altering the length will also increase the number of steps you'll need.

MATERIALS

Cut list:
- 4-foot (1¼-m) 1x10 (19 x 235-mm)
- Twelve 9¼-inch (24-cm) 1x1s (¾ x ¾-inch [19 x 19-mm])

Parts list:
- Two hooks
- Box of 1-inch (2½-cm) nails

Tools needed:
- Circular saw
- Table saw
- Electric drill
- Pin nailer or hammer
- Miter saw (optional)
- Tape measure
- Square

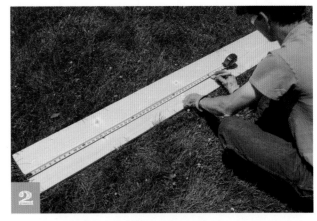

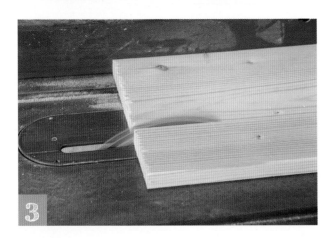

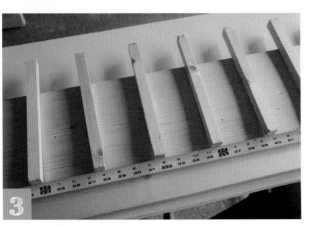

Step 1: Cut ramp

Use a circular saw to cut a 1x10 (19 x 235-mm) into a 4-foot (1¼-m) length.

Step 2: Mark steps

Next, use a tape measure, pencil, and square to mark where the steps will go on the 1x10 (19 x 235-mm). We're using 4-inch (10-cm) spacing for this example, which makes a total of twelve steps.

Step 3: Prepare steps

The steps will be made out of twelve 9¼-inch (24-cm) 1x1s (the actual dimensions are ¾ x ¾-inch [19 x 19 mm]). A table saw is the best way to make them; we used a 1x3 (19 x 64 mm), but you can use any piece of 1x (19-mm x) lumber that is long enough. Take care making the rips and keep your fingers away from the blade. First, use the table saw to cut long strips of 1x1s (19 x 19 mm) and then cut them to 9¼ inches (24 cm) with a miter saw or circular saw.

Step 4: Nail steps

An air-powered pin nailer is the quickest and easiest way to fasten the steps to the ramp, but you could predrill nail holes and use a hammer.

Step 5: Add hooks

Two simple hooks or eye hooks are needed on the top end of the ramp so that you can attach it to your coop (or whatever object your chickens need to access). You might be able to screw the hooks in by hand, or you may need to predrill the holes first. Then set up your ramp, and it will be ready for your chickens to use.

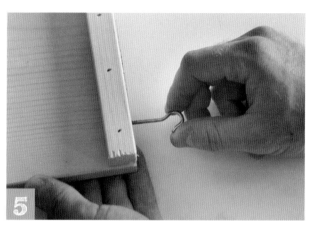

Chicken Swing

Level of Difficulty: Beginner
Length of Time: 1 hour

If you're looking for a simple project that's fun for you to make and fun for your chickens to use, you can't do much better than a chicken swing.

A chicken swing is basically just a roost that hangs from the ceiling of your chicken coop and is low enough so that the hens can easily hop on board and take a swing. Some hens may actually be able to create a bit of back-and-forth motion, or they may just use it as a place to hang out. In any case, the swing is easy to make and isn't a time-consuming project. There are many ways you could approach this project, but we'll show you one method that is particularly easy. The swing requires only a few materials.

As we mentioned, you have a lot of flexibility in this project. For the base of the swing, we used a piece of scrap wood that was actually intended to be a stair railing. It provides a nice shape that the hens should be able to easily grab. You can use another type of wood, even a "rustic" branch that still has the bark on it; choose whatever you like.

It may take a bit of time for the hens to get used to the swing, but once they become familiar with it, it should be a fun place for them to sit.

MATERIALS

Cut/parts list:
- Two 55-inch (1½-m) sections of ⅛-inch (3-mm) polypropylene rope
- Four 1¼ x 5/8-inch (32 x 16-mm) screw eyes
- 24-inch (61-cm) pine 2x2 (38 x 38 mm), rounded

Tools needed:
- Circular saw or hand saw
- Electric drill
- 7/64-inch (3-mm) drill bit or similar size as needed
- Utility knife or handheld snippers
- Matches
- Tape measure

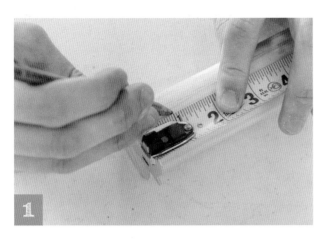

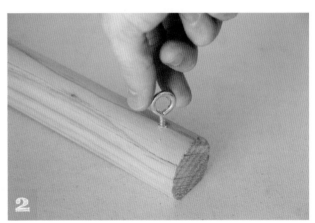

Step 1: Measure and cut swing base

Cut the wood into a 24-inch (61-cm) section (or a different length if needed for your coop). Measure and cut the section with a circular saw (or hand saw).

Step 2: Drill holes and attach screw eyes

Use a screw eye on each end of the wood to attach the rope to the swing base; we set each screw eye 1 inch (2½ cm) in from the ends of the swing base. Predrill the screw holes with a drill bit that is slightly smaller than the diameter of the screw; in our case, we used a ⁷⁄₆₄-inch (3-mm) drill bit. Predrilling makes the task of fastening the screw eyes very simple; you'll probably be able to do it by hand.

Step 3: Measure and cut rope

Next, cut two sections of rope with which to hang the swing. We used 55-inch (1½-m) pieces of ⅛-inch (3-mm) polypropylene clothesline, but your required length may be different. You basically want the swing to hang low enough that the chickens will be encouraged to easily hop up on it. Cut the rope to length and then lightly (and carefully!) burn the ends with a match to keep them from fraying. Tie a section of rope to each screw eye.

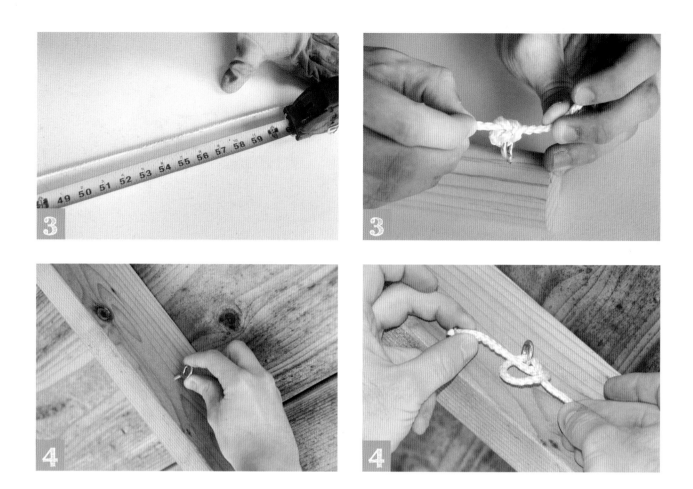

Step 4: Hang the swing

Take the swing to your coop for hanging. We attached the upper ends of the ropes right to the rafters by predrilling holes and then installing two additional screw eyes to hold the upper ends of the ropes. Keep the swing level as you install it.

Chicken Sweater

Level of Difficulty: Intermediate

Length of Time: 5 hours

Y ou know what they say about "all work and no play…" Not every project has to be serious or necessarily productive—sometimes a fun chicken-themed craft can be a nice diversion. This chicken sweater project is one of those fun projects. It's a great choice for those snowy winter afternoons when you'd like to be making something but don't feel inclined to work on a DIY project outside. Instead, curl up on the sofa and start knitting!

This is a fairly easy pattern, but does include a few techniques that might be difficult for a complete beginner. Because counting your rows and repetitions is so important, it's helpful to keep a pen and paper with you while you work so you can keep count easily and remember where you're at in the pattern if you have to leave the project for a while.

Note: Some chicken keepers caution against allowing chickens to wear sweaters due to possible disadvantages (inability to preen, for example). We suggest that you look at this project simply as a fun conversation piece ("What are you making?" "A chicken sweater!") rather than as a utilitarian item for your hens. Because even though your chickens don't need their very own sweaters, they sure are fun to make. The sweater can also make for a great photo op!

MATERIALS

Supplies needed:
- 1 or 2 balls (approximately 150 yards [137 m]) worsted weight yarn
- Size 6 (4-mm) knitting needles
- Yarn needle
- Velcro
- Sewing thread
- Sewing needle
- Scissors

Abbreviations used:

[ ]: Repeat these stitches as many times as specified.

inc: Increase. Start to make a normal knit stitch, but instead of slipping the loop off of your left-hand needle and leaving the stitch on your right-hand needle, slip the loop on your right-hand needle over the tip of your left-hand needle. This will create another stitch on your left-hand needle.

k: Knit

k2tog: Knit two together. Instead of putting your right-hand needle through one stitch on your left-hand needle, put it through two stitches and knit them as one. You'll be left with one stitch. This is also called a *decrease*.

p: Purl

p2tog: Purl two together. Instead of putting your right-hand needle through one stitch on your left-hand needle, put it through two stitches and purl them as one. You'll be left with one stitch. This is also called a *decrease*.

sts: Stitches

Sweater Front

Cast on 43 sts.

Row 1: k3, [p1, k1] to last 3 sts, k3.

Row 2: k3, [k1, p1] to last 3 sts, k3.

Repeat rows 1 and 2 twice.

Row 7: k3, [p1, k1] to last 3 sts, k3.

Row 8: Knit.

Row 9: k3, p to last 3 sts, k3.

Repeat rows 8 and 9 twice.

Row 14: k3, k2tog, k to last 5 sts, k2tog, k3. (41 sts)

Row 15: k3, p to last 3 sts, k3.

Row 16: Knit.

Repeat rows 15 and 16 twice.

Row 21: k3, p2tog, p to last 5 sts, p2tog, k3 (39 sts).

Repeat rows 8 to 21 three times. (27 sts).

Neck Opening and First Shoulder

Row 1: k11, cast off 5, k11. (22 sts)

You will now have eleven stitches for each shoulder. Work the shoulder nearest the end of your left-hand needle first, ignoring the other momentarily.

Row 2: k3, [p2tog] twice, p4. (9 sts)

Row 3: k2, [k2tog] twice, k3. (7 sts)

Row 4: k3, [p2tog] once, p2. (6 sts)

Row 5: Knit.

Row 6: k3, p3.

Row 7: Knit.

Row 8: k3, p3.

Row 9: Knit.

Row 10: k2, inc, k to end. (7 sts)

Row 11: k3, inc2, p to end. (9 sts)

Row 12: k3, inc2, k to end. (11 sts)

Row 13: k3, p to end.

Cut yarn, leaving a tail several inches long. You will now work the second shoulder.

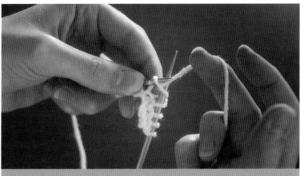

To increase, you just start to make a normal knit stitch...

...and slip the resulting loop over your left-hand needle instead of your right-hand needle.

Knitting two stitches together to decrease.

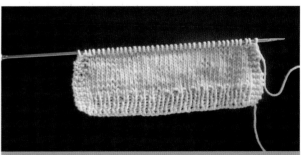

On the left side, you can see the effect of the decrease stitch. The current row is noticeably shorter than the last row.

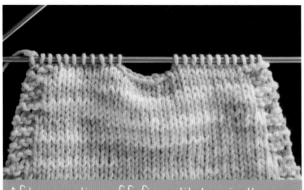

After casting off five stitches in the middle, you should have eleven stitches on either side of the neck opening; you will work them one at a time.

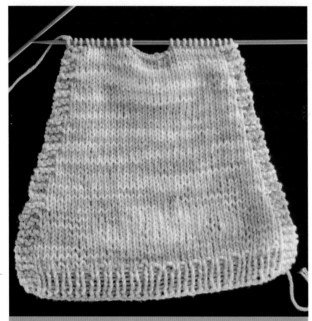

The sweater will be much wider at the bottom than at the neck opening. It should be about 8.5 inches (22 cm) long, bottom to top.

Second Shoulder

Row 1: p4, [p2tog] twice, k3. (9 sts)

Row 2: k3, [k2tog] twice, k2. (7 sts)

Row 3: p2, [p2tog] once, k3. (6 sts)

Row 4: Knit.

Row 5: p3, k3.

Row 6: Knit.

Row 7: p3, k3.

Row 8: Knit.

Row 9: k4, inc, k2. (7 sts)

Row 10: p4, inc2, k3. (9 sts)

Row 11: k6, inc2, k3. (11 sts)

Row 12: k3, p to end.

Row 13: Using the tail of yarn you left on the other shoulder, cast on 5 sts to your left-hand needle. P to last 3 sts, K3. (27 sts)

Row 14: Knit.

Sweater Back

At this point, you just begin reversing the instructions for the sweater front, increasing where you had been decreasing.

Row 1: k3, inc, p to last 3 sts, inc, k3. (29 sts)

Row 2: Knit.

Row 3: k3, p to last 3 sts, k3.

Repeat rows 2 and 3 twice.

Row 8: k3, inc, k to last 3 sts, inc, k3. (31 sts)

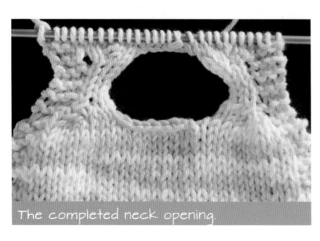

The completed neck opening.

Weave in the tail ends of your yarn.

Row 9: k3, p to last 3 sts, k3.

Row 10: Knit.

Repeat rows 9 and 10 twice.

Row 15: k3, inc, p to last 3 sts, inc, k3. (33 sts)

Repeat rows 1 to 15 three times. (43 sts).

Row 45: Cast on 5 sts. k3, [p1, k1] to end of row. Cast on 5 sts to your left-hand needle. p1, k1, k3. (53 sts)

Row 46: k3, [k1, p1] to last 3 sts, k3.

Row 47: k3, [p1, k1] to last 3 sts, k3.

Repeat rows 46 and 47 twice.

Cast off.

Finishing

Using your yarn needle, weave any yarn ends into your knitting and cut off the excess. Sew small squares of Velcro to the tabs on the back of the sweater and to the bottom corners of the front to create the "wing holes." Now your chicken can strut her stuff in a cozy chicken sweater (long enough for you to take a picture, anyway!).

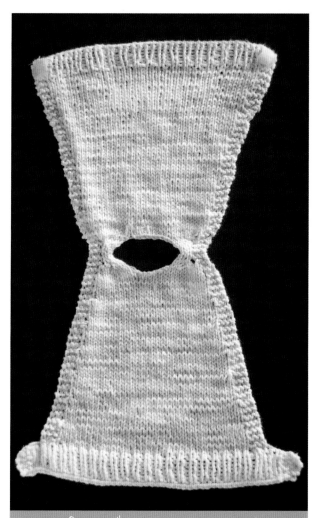

Almost finished! You can see the tabs at the bottom of the sweater where you will sew your Velcro.

The finished sweater! Your chicken should be able to use his wings freely while wearing the sweater, thanks to the large wing openings

Sew the Velcro so the tabs on the back of the sweater fasten over the front.

5-Gallon-Bucket Nest Boxes

Level of Difficulty: Beginner

Length of Time: 1 hour

If you have a lot of chickens in your flock or have plans to expand your numbers soon, you're going to need a lot of nest boxes. Even though some hens may take turns and happily share nest boxes, it can be helpful to have plenty of nest boxes to go around. You may soon find yourself asking, "Is there an inexpensive and simple way I can build extra nest boxes?" We're glad you asked, because a simple "in-a-pinch" nest box can be built from a basic 5-gallon (20-liter) bucket and is one of the easiest projects in the book. This is a great project for using up smaller, scrap-type materials, because the 2x4s (38 x 89 mm) are quite short, and the plywood piece is small. We'll show you how to build a frame for a 5-gallon (20-liter) bucket that will hold it in place, keep the eggs in, and mount easily inside your coop.

MATERIALS

Cut list:
- Two 14-inch (36-cm) 2x4s (38 x 89 mm)
- Two 17½-inch (44-cm) 2x4s (38 x 89 mm)
- 14 x 17½-inch (36 x 44-cm) piece of ½-inch (13-mm)-thick or ¾-inch (19-mm)-thick plywood

Parts list:
- Standard-size 5-gallon (20-liter) bucket
- Box of 3-inch (8-cm) screws
- Box of 1½-inch (4-cm) screws

Tools needed:
- Circular saw
- Miter saw (optional)
- Table saw (optional)
- Tape measure
- Electric drill
- Utility knife
- Wire snippers

Step 1: Make cuts

Begin by making the necessary cuts to your lumber. A miter saw will speed up the process of cutting the 2x4s (38 x 89 mm), but a circular saw will also do the job. Cut the plywood to size with a circular saw or table saw.

Step 2: Assemble box frame

Using the two 14-inch (36-cm) 2x4s (38 x 89 mm) as the front and back and the two 17½-inch (44-cm) 2x4s (38 x 89 mm) as the sides, construct a simple rectangle as shown in the photos. Use 3-inch (8-cm) screws to fasten.

Step 3: Attach base

Next, use 1½-inch (4-cm) screws to attach the plywood base to the rectangle frame and then flip the entire nest box frame over so the plywood is down.

Step 4: Remove bucket handle

To make the nest box safe for the hens, it's a good idea to remove the metal handle from the 5-gallon (20-liter) bucket. We were able to do this easily without tools.

Step 5: Fasten 5-gallon (20-liter) bucket

Place the handle-less bucket inside the frame. The 2x4 (38 x 89 mm) on the front provides a barrier that chickens can easily step over but that will keep eggs from rolling out. The frame also provides an easy way to fasten your new nest box to the wall of the coop.

Optional: Modify bucket lid

If you're in a hurry and not interested in building a wooden frame, you can simply modify the lid of the 5-gallon (20-liter) bucket to create the front of the nest box. To do this, use a scrap 2x4 (38 x 89 mm) as a guide to mark a pencil line across the bucket lid as shown, and then carefully score the line with a utility knife. You may need to use wire snippers to cut through the thickest parts of the lid. After making the cut, attach the modified lid to the bucket. One potential problem with this method is that the cut plastic lid may be uneven and rough, so take care to keep the edges smooth.

Egg Hod

Level of Difficulty: Intermediate
Length of Time: 2 hours

For many chicken owners, the birds themselves are interesting and fun, but a major attraction is the prospect of enjoying fresh eggs each day. It's easy to imagine yourself on a picture-perfect sunny morning, happily searching each nest box for eggs and collecting them to take inside for a farm-fresh breakfast. But wait a minute—-collecting the eggs into *what*? Naturally, you'll need a proper egg-collecting basket. And in the DIY spirit of this book, why not create your own egg basket using some simple materials and a small investment of time?

The basket we're going to make here is just one possibility of what you could design. Feel free to make modifications to the style and consider decorating or painting in whatever way you find appealing. The mesh we used for the bottom and sides of the basket is just wire window screen. This screen is easy to work with and strong, and it gives the basket a nice, clean look. Alternatively, you could use nylon screen, which is readily available and also very easy to work with.

MATERIALS

Cut list:
- Two 6 x 9-inch (15 x 23-cm) pieces of ¾-inch (19-mm) pine
- Two 18-inch (46-cm) ⅝-inch (16-mm) wooden rods
- 18-inch (46-cm) ¾-inch (19-mm) wooden rod
- 16½ x 16½-inch (42 x 42-cm) section of screen

Tools needed:
- Table saw or circular saw
- Electric drill
- Scissors or wire snippers
- Miter saw or circular saw
- Staple gun and staples
- Ruler or framing square
- Sandpaper
- Wood glue

Chicken DIY

Step 1: Prepare ends

Start off by using a table saw to cut two 6 x 9-inch (15 x 23-cm) pieces of ¾-inch (19-mm) pine (essentially, any piece of 1x [19 mm x] lumber wider than 6 inches [15 cm] will do the trick). Use a miter saw to cut two 45-degree angles at the top of each 6 x 9-inch (15 x 23-cm) piece as shown in the photos. Use sandpaper to nicely round off the edges.

Step 2: Drill hole for handle

Drill identical holes in each end piece for the handle. Predrill the hole first with a small bit and then use a ¾-inch (19-mm) bit to finish and make a hole large enough for the handle. The center of the hole should be about 1 inch (2½-cm) down from the top.

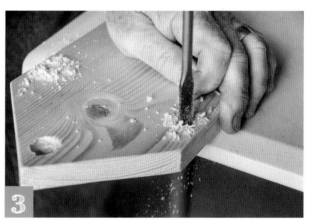

Step 3: Drill side holes

Smaller ⅝-inch (16-mm) rods are used for the sides of the basket and often come in 3-foot (91-cm) lengths, so cutting a 3-foot (91-cm) rod in half will give you the two 18-inch (46-cm) rods you'll need. Again, predrill the holes with a small bit and then use a ⅝-inch (16-mm) bit to finish. These holes should be ½ inch (13 mm) in from the sides and 4¾ inches up from the base, as shown in the photos.

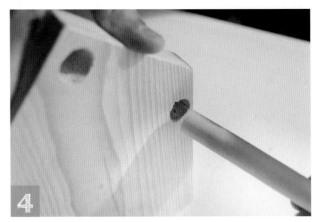

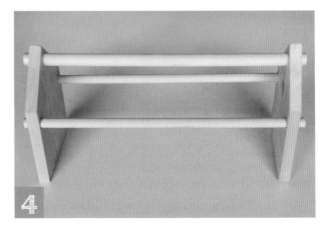

Step 4: Assemble basket frame

Carefully build the frame of the basket by combining the sides and the rods. They should fit together tightly, but still use wood glue to secure everything together. Each rod should extend through the hole about ½ inch (13 mm).

Step 5: Add screen

Use scissors or snippers to cut out a 16½ x 16½-inch (42 x 42-cm) section of screen. Use a ruler to fold about ½ inch over on each side to create a smooth finish, and then use staples to fasten the screen around the bottom and sides of the basket, as well as to the side rods. It helps to work in one direction and continually pull the screen taut as you go.

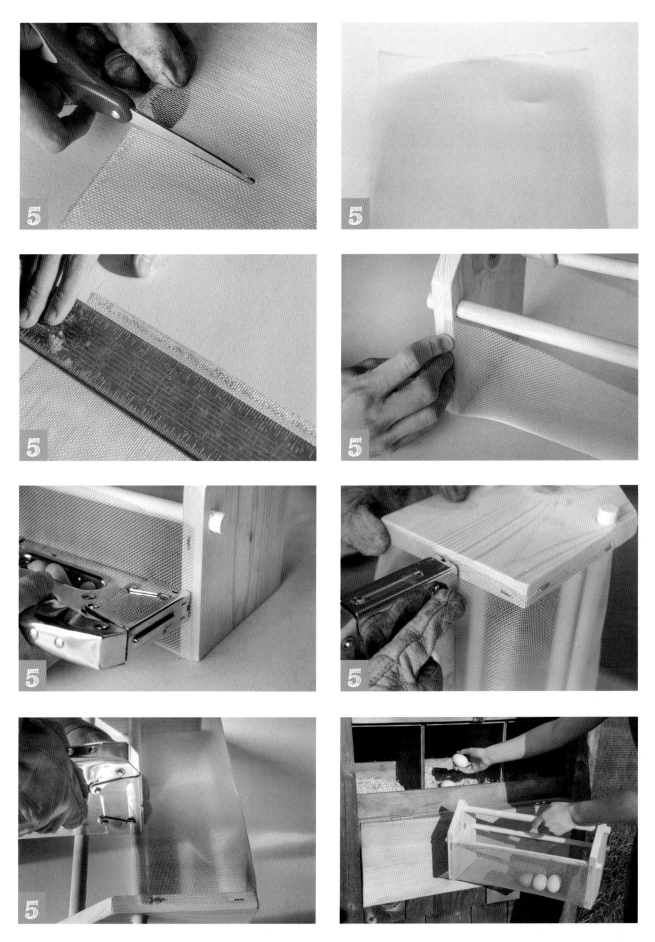

Grazing Box

Level of Difficulty: Beginner
Length of Time: 1 hour

I f you've been into chickens for a long time, you've likely observed two interesting facts regarding their grazing habits:

1. Chickens enjoy the opportunity to sample fresh green grasses and herbs.

2. Chickens often destroy these plants while trying to eat them!

Because chickens love to scratch and dig while eating, they often destroy the roots and soil of plants, and—over time—may turn any green areas to which they have access into sandy dirt pits with all of the plant roots destroyed. This can lead to chicken boredom, and it means that the chickens soon have no fresh plants to graze on.

A grazing box is one solution that can protect the plants while still allowing the chickens to access them. Simply place the finished grazing box on the ground inside your chicken run and then wait several days until the grass grows up through the hardware cloth. If the chickens have already decimated the soil there, you may need to rework the ground, or add topsoil, or possibly add grass seed. You can also plant chicken-friendly herbs such as oregano, mint, or lavender inside the grazing box. Once the plants come up through the wire, the chickens will be able to stand in the grazing box and munch on plants without ruining them. You can build as many grazing boxes as you need to meet your flock's needs, or you can modify the size of this version. Because this project requires fairly short segments of lumber, feel free to use scraps from other projects; this is what we did.

Note: For grasses, ¼-inch (6-mm) hardware cloth should work fine, but if you'd like to plant herbs for your chickens, you're probably better off with ½-inch (13-mm) hardware cloth so that the chickens will have an easier time reaching the leaves.

MATERIALS

Cut list:
- Two 21-inch (53-cm) cedar 2x4s (38 x 89 mm)
- Two 24-inch (61-cm) cedar 2x4s (38 x 89 mm)
- Two 21-inch (53-cm) cedar 2x2s (38 x 38 mm)
- Two 24-inch (61-cm) cedar 2x2s (38 x 38 mm)

Parts list:
- About 4 square feet ¼-inch (6-mm) or ½-inch (13-mm) hardware cloth (that's 2 x 2 feet [61 x 61 cm], but we'll actually be using 23½ x 23½ inches [60 x 60 cm])
- 3½-inch (9-cm) exterior screws
- Staples
- Wood glue

Tools list:
- Circular saw or other saw
- Electric drill
- Framing square
- Stapler
- Wire snippers

Step 1: Assemble main frame

Using the two 24-inch (61-cm) 2x4s (38 x 89 mm) and the two 21-inch (53-cm) 2x4s (38 x 89 mm), construct a simple 2 x 2-foot (61 x 61-cm) square as shown in the photos; the shorter 21-inch (53-cm) 2x4s (38 x 89 mm) go "inside" the longer 24-inch (61-cm) ones to ensure that the final frame is 2 feet (61 cm) square. Using wood glue and 3½-inch (9-cm) screws, fasten the 2x4s (38 x 89 mm) together (use a framing square to help keep the corners accurate).

Step 2: Attach hardware cloth

Using wire snippers, carefully cut a 23½ x 23½-inch (60 x 60-cm) square of hardware cloth (wear gloves and eye protection). Keeping the hardware cloth about ½ inch (13 mm) short on each side like this will ensure that it doesn't overlap the frame, as shown in the photos. A stapler is a fast and easy way to attach the hardware cloth, but you can also use short nails with large heads, such as roofing nails, to get the job done.

Step 3: Add trim

The chickens will be climbing up onto the top of the grazing box to use it, so adding some trim to the top of the box will keep the chickens away from the sharp edges of the hardware cloth. We used 2x2s (38 x38 mm) for this job, two of them cut to 24 inches (61 cm) and two of them cut to 21 inches (53 cm). Using more 3½-inch (9-cm) exterior screws, build a square over the first one, using the 2x2s (38 x38 mm) to cover up the edge of the hardware cloth.

Step 4: Placement

Place the grazing box in an area that your chickens frequent and then wait a few days for the grass to come up through the hardware cloth.

Wading Pool

Level of Difficulty: Intermediate

Length of Time: 2 hours

When hot summer weather hits your location, your hens will likely begin searching for ways to stay cool, just like everyone else. Thankfully, there are a few ways that you can help keep your chickens comfortable in the heat. For example, you can provide shady spots, make sure that the chickens have access to cool ground that they can scratch up and lie in, and put ice in their water to help lower its temperature. Another hen-cooling option: a wading pool!

A simple children's wading pool (we used one with a 3½-foot [1-m] diameter) can be repurposed into a chicken pool with little effort, but you may find that the chickens are reluctant to climb in. So for this project, we included instructions for building a small ramp that the chickens can use to climb in and out of the water.

You may experience mixed results with this project. Some chickens enjoy the water and will wade in, get their feet wet, and even swim, while other chickens will want nothing to do with standing water and will ignore the pool.

An important thing to keep in mind is that *the water should not be deep.* Don't fill the pool more than a few inches at most, because it is possible that a chicken could drown in deeper water. The main idea is for the chickens to simply walk in the water, get a little bit wet, and stay cool on a hot summer day. You can also place small rocks or pebbles on the floor of the pool to help keep the water shallow.

MATERIALS

Cut list:
- Two 2-foot (61-cm) 1x10s (19 x 235 mm)
- Ten 9¼-inch (24-cm) 1x1s (¾ x ¾ inch [19 x 19 x 19 mm])

Parts list:
- 42-inch (1-m)-diameter plastic wading pool
- Two 2-inch (5-cm) hinges
- Box of 1-inch (2½-cm) nails

Tools needed:
- Table saw
- Circular saw
- Electric drill
- Pin nailer or hammer
- Tape measure
- Square
- Miter saw (optional)

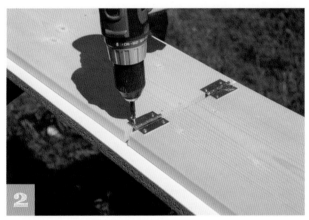

Step 1: Prepare ramps

Use a circular saw to cut two 2-foot (61-cm) 1x10s (19 x 235 mm), which you will use for the ramp leading in and out of the pool. One way to obtain the ramp pieces is by purchasing an 8-foot (2½-m) 1x10 (19 x 235 mm), cutting it into two 4-foot (1¼-m) pieces, and then cut one of those 4-foot (1¼-m) pieces into two 2-foot (61-cm) pieces. This leaves you with a remaining 4-foot (1¼-m) piece to use for another project—perhaps a standard chicken ramp.

Step 2: Fasten hinges

Join the 1x10s (19 x 235 mm) together with two 2-inch (5-cm) hinges. Predrilling the screw holes can be helpful. Try to keep the hinges as straight as possible so that the two sides of the ramp fold up neatly when not in use. After attaching both hinges, flip the ramp over so that the hinges face down and will bend properly to allow the ramp to fit over the side of the wading pool.

Step 3: Prepare steps

The chickens will appreciate something to grip as they climb the ramp, and that's what the ten 9¼-inch (24-cm) 1x1s are for (remember, the actual dimensions are ¾ x ¾-inch [19 x 19 mm]). A table saw is the best way to make them; we used a 1x3 (19 x 64 mm), but you can use any piece of 1x (19 mm x) lumber that is long enough. Take care while making the rips and keep your fingers away from the blade. First, use the table saw to cut long strips of 1x1s and then cut them to 9¼ inches (24 cm) with a circular or miter saw.

Step 4: Nail steps

An air-powered pin nailer is the quickest and easiest way to fasten the steps to the ramp; alternatively, you could predrill nail holes and use a hammer. Place the steps either on 4-inch (10-cm) centers (at 4, 8, 12, 16, and 20 inches [10, 20, 30½, 41, and 51 cm]) or position each step so that there is a distance of 3⅜ inches (9 cm) between each one. You won't need steps on the very bottom or very top of each ramp. Remember that the hinges need to be facing down when you nail on the steps. Use a square to help you make the steps straight.

Step 5: Set up and use

Place the wading pool in a spot where the chickens can access it. Fill it with a small amount of water and then set the hinged ramp over one side of the pool so that the chickens can easily climb in and out.

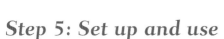

Recipes for Egg-cess Eggs

Level of Difficulty: Intermediate
Length of Time: Varies

After all your hard work, it's time for your hens to give something back, and that means fresh eggs every day. But an ironic thing often happens to chicken keepers after a while: they end up with *too many* eggs—more than they can use! So if you find yourself with delicious, farm-fresh eggs coming out your ears, don't let these *egg-cess* eggs go to waste—put them to good use in the kitchen.

Unfortunately, a pair of fried eggs with your toast at breakfast isn't the most efficient way to use up all those eggs, which is why you need *egg-ceptional* recipes that utilize plenty of *egg-stra* eggs; recipes that give you plenty of bang for your buck—er, make that *cluck*. When you think of egg-centric recipes, you probably think of dishes like quiche or pound cake—recipes that traditionally call for high quantities of eggs. But maybe you'd like to try your hand at something a little different. In that case, read on and acquaint yourself with these recipes that not only use up plenty of eggs but also transform mealtime from humdrum to *egg-citing*.

Double Cheese Farmhouse Frittata

It's easy, it's cheesy, and it's palate-pleasing—this yummy frittata uses eight eggs and is a hearty, filling dish that everybody will love. We've included a basic recipe here, but you can also add in your favorite optional ingredients: ham, tomatoes, bacon, spinach, quinoa—you name it!

Ingredients:

- 8 eggs
- 1 medium to large onion, chopped
- 1 sweet pepper, chopped
- 3 tablespoons (1½ oz or 43 g) butter
- ¾ cup (⅕ liter) milk
- 1½ cups (6 oz or 168 g) cheddar cheese, shredded
- ½ teaspoon salt
- ¼ teaspoon pepper
- ¼ teaspoon basil leaves
- ¾ cup (3 oz or 85 g) mozzarella cheese, shredded

Directions:

1. In a skillet, sauté the onions and sweet pepper in butter until the onions are clear. Transfer the vegetables to the bottom of an 8 x 8-inch (20 x 20-cm) baking dish.

2. In a bowl, whisk the eggs, milk, cheddar cheese, salt, pepper, and basil. Pour the egg mixture over the vegetables.

3. Bake at 350°F (177°C) for 40 minutes or until the eggs are firm, and then sprinkle the mozzarella cheese on top and bake for another 5 to 10 minutes. Serve hot.

Serves 4 to 6

Delightful Deviled Eggs

How do we love deviled eggs? Let us count the ways…. If you like a mix of spicy and sweet flavors, you'll love this version with the addition of sweet pepper.

Ingredients:

- 5 eggs, hard-boiled and peeled
- ¼ cup (2 oz or 58 g) mayonnaise
- 1 teaspoon mustard
- ½ teaspoon parsley flakes
- ½ teaspoon chopped chives
- ⅛ teaspoon cayenne pepper
- Black pepper to taste
- Orange bell pepper, chopped into ½-inch (1¼-cm) pieces (to garnish)
- Paprika (optional)

Directions:

1. Slice the eggs in half lengthwise and then gently scoop out the yolks. Place the yolks in a small bowl and mash well with a fork.

2. Add the mayonnaise and mustard to the yolks and mix thoroughly. Add the parsley flakes, chopped chives, cayenne pepper, and black pepper and continue to mix.

3. Place the egg-yolk mixture in a pastry bag or a zip-top bag (clip the corner so that you can pipe the mixture through the hole). Pipe the mixture back into each egg white, filling the empty space.

4. Garnish each egg with a small piece of orange bell pepper and then sprinkle with paprika if desired.

Makes 10

Triple Chocolate Torte

Here's what you need to know about this recipe: (1) it's gluten free, (2) it's delicious served warm or cold, and (3): it's one of the most superb things you'll ever eat.

Ingredients:

- 6 eggs
- 1½ sticks (¾ cup/6 oz/170 g) salted butter
- 2 cups (12 oz or 300 g) bittersweet baking chocolate
- ½ cup (3½ oz or 100 g) sugar
- ⅛ teaspoon vanilla
- ½ cup (3 oz or 75 g) semisweet chocolate chips
- ¾ cup (3¼ oz or 105 g) unsweetened cocoa powder or confectioner's sugar

Directions:

1. Butter the bottom and sides of a 9-inch (23-cm) springform pan and dust with a small amount of the cocoa powder. Set the remaining cocoa powder aside to dust the top of the torte later.

2. In a medium saucepan over medium-low heat, melt the butter and baking chocolate, stirring constantly, until combined. Set aside to cool for a few minutes.

3. In a mixing bowl, beat together the eggs, sugar, and vanilla; whisk until thoroughly combined.

4. Slowly add the chocolate mixture to the egg mixture and whisk together well, and then stir in the chocolate chips.

5. Pour the batter into the springform pan and place it in a preheated 350°F (177°C) oven for 50 minutes or until firm.

6. Remove from pan once the torte has cooled, and then dust the top with the remainder of the cocoa powder (or confectioner's sugar).

Serves 10

Homemade Whipped Cream

You can make your own whipped cream by combining 1 cup of heavy cream, ½ cup (4 oz or 114 g) of sour cream, and ¼ cup (1 oz or 35 g) of confectioner's sugar using an electric mixer. Beat until stiff peaks form. Serve with torte.

Honey Nut Custard

Honey and cinnamon combine with the goodness of eggs to create this old-fashioned custard. Toss in some toasted almonds for added crunch.

Ingredients:

- 6 eggs
- ½ cup (6 oz or 170 g) wildflower honey
- ¼ teaspoon cinnamon
- ¼ teaspoon salt
- 1½ cups (¾-pint) half-and-half
- 1 cup (⅖ pint) milk
- ¾ cup (3¾ oz or 105 g) toasted almonds (bake in a 350°F [177°C] oven for 10 minutes, stirring halfway through)

Directions:

1. In a medium bowl, whisk together the eggs, honey, cinnamon, and salt. Slowly add the half-and-half and milk, and then whisk to combine all ingredients.

2. Pour the mixture into 8 ramekins, stopping ½ to ¾ inch (13 to 19 mm) from the top. Place the ramekins in a large roasting pan and fill the pan with hot water until it reaches about halfway up the side of the ramekins.

3. Lightly cover the roasting pan with aluminum foil and bake in a 350° F [177°C] oven for one hour or until set.

4. Serve warm or cold, topped with toasted almonds for a nice crunch. Other tasty toppings include berries and coconut flakes.

Serves 8

Lovely Lemon Curd

This lemon curd is smooth, satiny, and perfect for a variety of uses. You could include it as a filling for cupcakes or shortbread cookies; pour it over berries; spread it on muffins, French toast, or biscuits; or serve with scones. You can also try this recipe with another citrus fruit, such as lime or orange, in place of the lemon. Yum!

Ingredients:

- 3 large eggs, plus 3 additional egg yolks, beaten together
- 1¼ sticks (⅗ cup or 5 oz or 142 g) butter
- 1½ cups (10½ cups or 300 g) sugar
- 1 cup (½ pint) freshly squeezed lemon juice (about 4 to 6 large lemons)
- ¼ cup (⅘ oz or 24 g) lemon zest

Directions:

1. Place the butter, sugar, lemon juice, lemon zest, and eggs in a medium to large saucepan. Cook over medium-low heat for approximately 5 minutes, stirring constantly—do not let the mixture get too hot or boil. Lower the heat a bit if needed and continue to stir the mixture for approximately 5 to 8 more minutes, until it thickens and reads about 170°F (77°C) on a thermometer.

2. Set a strainer over a bowl and slowly pour the mixture through the strainer and into the bowl. Place plastic wrap on the surface of the curd to prevent it from forming a skin while it cools.

3. Once the curd is cooled, you can place it in an airtight container and refrigerate for 2 to 3 weeks. The lemon curd will continue to thicken in the fridge.

Makes 2 cups (1 pint)

Bacon, Egg, and Cheese Crumble

If you need to feed a crowd, try this hearty combination of bacon, eggs, and cheese. It makes a filling and delicious dish that packs plenty of goodness into every single bite.

Ingredients:

- 10 eggs, hardboiled, peeled, and sliced
- ¾ stick (6 tablespoons or 3 oz or 85 g) butter
- 2 tablespoons flour
- 1½ cups (¾ pint) half-and-half
- ½ teaspoon salt
- ¼ teaspoon pepper
- ¾ cup (6 oz or 150 g) cheddar cheese, cut into small pieces
- 12 strips of cooked bacon, crumbled
- Cracker crumbs (crumble 20–25 crackers)

Directions:

1. In a medium saucepan, start to prepare the cheese sauce by melting the butter, and then add the flour slowly so no lumps form. Gradually add the half-and-half and cook over low heat until it thickens a bit—about 10 minutes.

2. Add the salt, pepper, and cheese. Stir until the cheese is fully melted, and then remove the cheese sauce from heat.

3. In a 9 x 9-inch (23 x 23-cm) pan, layer half of the eggs, followed by half of the crumbled bacon and half of the cheese sauce. Repeat the layers again.

4. Sprinkle the cracker crumbs over the top and bake at 350° F [177°C] for about 40 minutes.

Serves 6 to 8

(Still) Got Eggs?

Need more ideas? Try these additional ideas for dishes that require a lot of eggs:

- Soufflé
- Omelet
- Quiche
- Egg noodles
- Mousse
- Pound and angel-food cake
- Pudding
- Ice cream
- Egg salad
- Eggnog
- Brioche dough
- Homemade mayonnaise

It's also very simple to freeze eggs. Just crack the eggs into a bowl, gently stir until blended, and pour into freezer containers. Mark the container with the number of eggs and the date, and the eggs will keep in the freezer for about a year.

Index

Photo Credits

All photos copyright Daniel Johnson, Fox Hill Photo (www.foxhillphoto.com), unless otherwise noted below.

Additional photographs provided by:

Front cover: The Len/Shutterstock (top left), Vickspix/Shutterstock (top right), chasdesign/Shutterstock (center left), Elliot Photography/Shutterstock (center right)

Title page: Jenny Swab/Shutterstock

Hen and rooster illustration (1, 4, 8, 14, 19, 26, 32, 34, 42, 48, 58, 68, 76, 82, 88, 94, 100, 106, 114, 122, 128, 134, 142, 148, 156, 162, 168, 186, 192): Anastasia Zenina-Lembrik/Shutterstock

Background for Materials pages (31, 45, 51, 61, 71, 79, 85, 91, 97, 103, 109, 117, 125, 131, 137, 145, 151, 159, 165): donatas1205/Shutterstock

Notepad graphic for Materials pages (31, 45, 51, 61, 71, 79, 85, 91, 97, 103, 109, 117, 125, 131, 137, 145, 151, 159, 165): Andy Dean Photography/Shutterstock

Background for sidebars (19, 22, 24, 47, 56, 60, 62, 63, 65, 73, 78, 119, 176, 184): NatBasil/Shutterstock

Daniel Johnson author photo, 192: J. Keeler Johnson

Shutterstock: Alonafoto, 144; Dmytro Amanzholov, 161 (left); Anneka, 83; A_noina, 82; Nagy-Bagoly Arpad, 19; BankBaht, 89; beerlogoff, 108; Josipa Bjelobrk, 96; Elena Blokhina, 102, 103 (bottom), 105; NatalyaBond, 95; JurateBuiviene, 59; CapturePB, 20 (tape measure); CK Foto, 167 (water graphic); critterbiz, 136; cynoclub, 119; Djem, 128; Elena Elisseeva, 58, 60; etorres, 184 (left) ; Iakov Filimonov, 150; Thada Fuangnakhon, 22 (nails); Miroslaw Gierczyk, 15; Gitanna, 137 (knitting needle); gresei, 168; grzym, 158; HelloRF Zcool, 164; indigolotos, 63 (gloves); kml, 76, 143; Roman Kosolapov, 24; Holly Kuchera, 25; Lamzinvnikola, 157; lantapix, 124; Robert F. Leahy, 184 (right) ; The Len, 27; Oleksandr Lytvynenko, 112, 116; Mega Pixel, 20 (orange pencil); Kostikova Natalia, 138; Olhastock, 70; Rawpixel.com, 169; Red Tiger, 187; Venera Salman, 68; schankz, 91 (chicken); senk, 190; sevenke, 115; shapovalphoto, 101; Oksana Shufrych, 18 (second from top); Mariya Siyanko, 171; sjk2012, 32; stockphoto mania, 121 (left); SunshineItaly, 185; Alexander Sviridov, 106; Val Thoermer, 8; Timmary, 153 (bottom); Valerie Tonu, 33; Popova Valeriya, 133 (bottom); Chepko Danil Vitalevich, 3; Hong Vo, 6; Yvonne Wierink, 134; xpixel, 44; Yunaval, 17 (second from bottom);

About the Authors

Brother-and-sister collaborators **Samantha Johnson** and **Daniel Johnson** pursue their writing, photography, and agricultural interests at the family-owned Fox Hill and Pine Valley Farms in northern Wisconsin. Since 1999, they have raised and shown registered Welsh Mountain ponies, and they also enjoy the company of the several hundred thousand honey bees at Fox Hill and Pine Valley.

Samantha is an award-winning writer, as well as a proofreader and pony wrangler. She is a certified show judge with the Wisconsin State Horse Council and the Welsh Pony and Cob Society of America. She has written multiple books, including several on rabbits and a beginning vegetable-gardening guide (coauthored with Daniel). Samantha also enjoys fulfilling the demands of her bossy Corgi, Peaches.

Writer and photographer Daniel likes to spend his time lugging around heavy camera equipment in all kinds of weather to take pictures of everything from dogsledding in freezing temperatures to hay-baling in the heat of summer. He loves to photograph horses as well and is the coauthor (with Samantha) and photographer of several horse books. In his spare time, he also photographs frogs, one of which has been his pet for more than twenty-five years.